This book is dedicated to my teacher, Felix Klein,
whose professionalism, sensitivity, and generosity of spirit
ignited my love for graphology;

to Roger Rubin,
my mentor and dear colleague,
whose brilliance helped sustain it;

and to my late husband, Jack,
whose love helped provide support for it.

— ARLYN IMBERMAN

Contents

Acknowledgments

THIS IS A BOOK THAT WAS BUILT on the wisdom and assistance of many people for whom I express my great appreciation. I wish to thank the National Society of Graphology, where I studied for three intellectually stimulating years, and, in particular, Janice Klein, and my special colleagues, Maresi deMonchy, Adam Brand, Erik Rees, Madeleine Blanquefort d' Anglards, John Beck, Carole Schuler, Evie Tishelman, Irene Lawrence, Harriette Dekker, and, in addition, Peggy Kahn, Sheila Lowe, Dr. Ellen Bowers, and John Schlimm for their generosity in supplying me with some of their personal handwriting samples.

Many thanks to June Rifkin, my dear and valued coauthor; to Nanette Rousseau, my loyal, long-time assistant, for tracking down endless quotes and handwriting samples; and to Stanley Fisher, Ph.D., and Susan Leder for their valuable critiques.

I am also grateful to my agent, Peter Rubie, and Dorothy O'Brien, my editor at Andrews McMeel, for their competence and guidance and for encouraging me to write about the many aspects of graphology's reach that are reflected in these pages.

I am immensely appreciative of many friends who helped and stood by me from the beginning to the end of this project: Amy Shoen, Helene Benado, Constance Fairstone, and, in particular, Janine Gordon, for reading and discussing many of the chapters with me, and for her intelligence, clarity, and focus.

I am particularly indebted to Frieda Goldsmith, my most special friend, who showed her sustaining love and goodwill during my many years of research and writing; and to Nieka Fisher for guidance and assistance far beyond the call of duty.

Finally, I am grateful to numerous people who cannot be thanked by name—men and women whose writing appears in this book and whose privacy I have promised to protect. The book would not exist without them.

Foreword

By Ben Cohen
CEO, Ben & Jerry's Ice Cream

Encountering Arlyn Imberman and having her analyze my handwriting without our having met was an experience. As an entrepreneur, I'm always interested in cutting-edge tools that could be advantageous in providing information about people I am considering hiring. While I knew that much of what Arlyn shared with me about my writing could be public knowledge, there was also a great deal of specific information she conveyed that only someone close to me could have known.

For many years, I felt that going through a hiring process was as random as throwing résumés in the air and picking those that landed in a certain spot. Many times this resulted in hiring people who were not a good "fit" for the management style required or the culture of the company. Next time around I'm thinking that graphology is a discipline that could prove quite resourceful to our business and provide guidance in making better decisions overall. This experience was certainly a trip for me, and I'm pleased that Arlyn will be available for future consultations.

If you're not lucky enough to have your handwriting personally analyzed by Arlyn, this book should be the next best thing. You'll learn how handwriting reveals distinct personality types, both at the office and among your friends and family, and how to get along with them. You'll also closely examine the writings of many famous people in history, business, and entertainment, and gain insight as to what makes them successful. And finally, you'll even learn a thing or two about yourself.

Believe it or not, there are even more handwriting styles than varieties of ice cream! So, get ready to embark on a fascinating journey with *Signature for Success* as your guide.

Disclaimers

THE READER OF THIS BOOK should bear in mind that no reproduction of handwriting can ever fully convey the emotional quality, vitality, and pressure of the original document.

Throughout this book, for simplicity and brevity, the authors have used the personal pronouns *he, his, him,* and *himself* to refer to both males and females.

This book contains the opinions and ideas of its authors. It is intended to provide helpful and informative material on the subject matter covered. It is sold with the understanding that the authors and publisher are not engaged in rendering professional services in the book. If the reader requires personal assistance or advice, a competent professional should be consulted.

The authors and publisher specifically disclaim any responsibility for any liability, loss, or risk, personal or otherwise, which is incurred as a consequence, directly or indirectly, of the use and application of any of the contents of this book.

Some handwriting samples in this book have been reduced to meet formatting requirements.

Introduction

I CALL THEM GRAPHO-SKEPTICS. Like most Americans, they think graphology, the study of handwriting analysis, is a parlor game—a handy alternative to the Ouija board, or a close cousin of fortune-telling, palmistry, astrology, and phrenology. They show me samples of their handwriting and expect me to deliver some vague, safe generalities—nothing demonstrably false, but nothing terribly specific either. Then I tell them details about their character that even their spouses or close friends do not know, and hopefully without sounding too self-serving, I describe the intimate dynamics of their relationship with their parents. "Who told you that?" is the grapho-skeptic's favorite question. I always respond the same way: I point to their handwriting sample and say, "You did."

On one particular occasion, the grapho-skeptic in question, the CEO of a thriving investment banking boutique, was seated to my left at a dinner party. When I told him what I did for a living, he gave me the amused, condescending look I'm so used to seeing. Taking out his business card, he scribbled a sentence on the back. "Analyze this," he commanded. "If I like it, I'll throw you more business than you can handle."

A few days later, I could not resist delivering a three-page analysis of that one sentence. I showed him how his writing revealed his desire to dominate situations, his impatience with people who could not keep pace with his intelligence, his need to be surrounded by those who were not afraid to challenge him or to ask tough questions. We also spoke about why he had trouble sustaining close relationships with women.

"Okay, I'm convinced," he said, when he called me the next day. "Though I still wonder if you've been talking to my ex-wife."

He then hired me to help him learn more about his colleagues, his relationships to others, and himself. And that, when you get right down to it, is what I do for a living. I use my skills as a professional graphologist and executive coach to empower my clients and to give them the certainty they need to make the right hire, cut the best deal, or simply better understand the most important relationships in their lives.

٭   ٭   ٭

Why is graphology such an important tool in the workplace and in our personal lives? *Handwriting analysis?* you wonder. Perhaps, as it does for the grapho-skeptic, that very term conjures up for you images of crystal balls, palmistry, and zodiac charts. You are not alone in your perception! But the truth is, there is nothing New Agey about it. Graphology has been studied and practiced for centuries, and its roots are based in psychology and science. You may be surprised to learn that graphology is seriously used in investigative work, business, and counseling. Fortune 500 companies, police departments, colleges, and other respected institutions and businesses have benefited from its applications.

Our "handwriting" is made up of symbols we put down on paper. How each of us creates these symbols is what makes it so fascinating . . . and revealing. Our handwriting is uniquely ours: an imprint as singular as a fingerprint, and a key to our individuality.

Before my own study of graphology, I would make judgments about people, based on first impressions, which proved to be a superficial and often inaccurate method. Handwriting analysis offers a more reliable and objective way to assess personality and potential for greatness or dishonor, educational and personal achievement, parenting and interpersonal skills, romantic and business compatibility, or entrepreneurial and leadership traits. Graphology arrives at its ultimate assessment by uncovering not only the writer's "public" face but also what lies behind the mask—insights that speak to a person's *character*.

Relationships are seldom what they seem. As the American screenwriter Frances Marion said: "Do we really know anybody? Who does not wear one face to hide another?" While the average person can only surmise about what makes another person tick, a professional graphologist can tell us much, much more.

The best data gatherer and all-around computer in existence is the human mind, that "subconscious psychologist" which exists in all of us and has evolved from generations of experience in interpersonal evaluation. When we write, that subconscious is revealed by how we create those strokes and slants, and graphology helps us decipher these personal codes.

Freud believed it's impossible for anyone to keep a secret, but in actuality, when it comes to self-protection, people can be quite adept at keeping things hidden. And when we suddenly discover that a person we thought we knew turns out to be not who we think he is, it is shocking and disturbing. How do you reach inside to unlock the combination that defines another person? How can we understand more about another to foster compatibility, communication, and closeness? How can we lift the haze surrounding another soul? And what do we learn about ourselves in the process? Graphology is a tool to aid you in the journey of self-discovery, as well as the discovery and understanding of those with whom you live and work.

Though we've managed to accumulate considerable knowledge about ourselves, few of us are aware of how much we know. Therefore, the study of graphology, along with other techniques of personality assessment, turns out to be a matter of simply discovering the sources in others and ourselves that have always existed but been unknown and untapped. It is a single, direct, and immediate way in which one's weaknesses and blind spots can be discovered.

In the course of reading this book, you'll learn how to look at a writing pattern and decode it as professional graphologists do. You will examine the spacing, movement of letters, form of connection, margin, slant, signature, and much, much more.

You will also recognize how to achieve compatibility with a mate, friend, business partner, professional adviser, a team or family member. And, because the book is replete with illustrations of handwritings, along with charts and checklists, you will gain a better understanding of yourself and others with whom you come in contact.

This book is merely a first step, but I hope one that helps you begin discovering a discipline that will bring you insight and enjoyment in revealing the hidden traits and emotions that make up that fascinating enigma, the human personality.

Arlyn Imberman

NEW YORK CITY, 2003

CHAPTER 1

Writes of Passage

* * *

AN INTRODUCTION TO GRAPHOLOGY

*This chapter discusses the global use of graphology
as an accurate diagnostic tool in assessing personality and
human potential. A brief history of graphology is presented, along
with its various "schools" in Europe. The chapter concludes with a look
at how graphology is used in the business world, and what
the future holds, especially now that people write less
and use computers more.*

THE CLUES TO CHARACTER are everywhere: on a shopping list taped to the refrigerator . . . in the birthday cards you receive . . . on the note your boss left on your desk or a friend passed to you in class . . . even on your paycheck. Every day, everywhere, handwritten notes, letters, and signatures cross your path, and you've probably been unaware of the fascinating insights they hold. Until now.

Handwriting is a remarkable reflection of a person's true, but often "hidden," character, revealing things about personality, aptitudes, emotions, and state of mind beyond what can be observed in superficial actions or words. Learning to "read" the hidden character in handwriting not only helps you understand others but also is a valuable tool for self-discovery.

The use and application of handwriting analysis is called *graphology. Graph* comes from the Greek word *graphe,* which means "writing," and *ology* means "the study of."

Graphology has been seriously practiced for centuries throughout Europe. In America, businesses, universities, and government bureaus often retain the services of qualified graphologists to learn more about employees and students, as well as to uncover vital details in criminal investigations.

In everyday life, graphology can be used for personal and professional benefits—for yourself and in relationship to others. When you learn more about the secret language of handwriting and what it reveals, you'll gain insight into

- uncovering your hidden talents and skills
- recognizing inner strengths and weaknesses, hopes and fears
- discovering how compatible you are with others
- recognizing signs of conflict, anger, anxiety, and melancholy
- identifying romantic possibilities . . . or people to avoid
- seeing who's being honest with you . . . and who's not
- hiring the right person for the job and other useful applications

Best of all, this is knowledge that can be derived in a subtle and discreet manner.

The ABC's of Individuality

Think back to your childhood—say the first grade, or whenever you learned to write. Remember how you had to copy each letter of the alphabet—capital letters and small ones—using the standard copybook format that all school-age children are given? Once you learned your A's, B's, and C's, and began connecting the letters to create words and sentences, you probably noticed that even though you and your classmates were learning the same techniques in the same manner at the same time, your handwritings were not alike at all! You may have thought your penmanship was beautiful and perfect—just like the template you copied from. But Jonathan's writing was different—his letters seemed to be crammed together. Danny wrote so hard you could see indentations through the back of his page. Sarah's handwriting was large with big loops, while Carmen's was smaller and rounded and didn't have much of a slant. You wondered: How can that be? How can we learn to write the same letters the same way but have our writing turn out to be so different?

Since handwriting—and the skills of creating letters on the page—comes from our deeper self, it contains a great deal of information about our *character*. Whenever we write, our immediate emotions, moods, or state of mind influence our expression on paper. Our brain transmits this information to the motor reflexes in our hand. Therefore, our handwriting is a unique combination of our conscious and unconscious thoughts and feelings. Our handwriting reflects our personality in a way that is similar to our facial expressions, speech, and body language. It is, in essence, body language on paper.

The slants, strokes, size, pressure, and speed with which our pen glides on a page create this window to the soul. As we change and mature, so does our writing. Haven't you noticed the changes in your handwriting over the years, or even from day to day, depending on your mood or health?

The qualities in handwriting and its relationship to the writer have been studied for centuries, and they continue to hold fascination for psychologists, writers, philosophers, legal professionals, historians, and anyone else seeking deeper knowledge of the human character and condition.

The History of Graphology in a Nutshell

Beware of the man whose writing is always like a reed in the wind.

—CONFUCIUS

From prehistoric times, when early man began painting on cave walls through Egyptian hieroglyphics and to the early alphabets of the Greeks and Romans, there has always been interest in the relationship between the art of writing and the character of the writer.

Aristotle, the Greek philosopher, observed that writing styles were as unique to each individual as his or her speaking voice. He even studied the link between the writer and his handwriting.

The Roman historian, Gaius Suetonius Tranquillus noted that Emperor Augustus Caesar did not separate his words well on paper, which implied that he was unwilling to let go of money, material things, and his own feelings.

Camillo Baldi (1550–1637), a physician and educator, and dean of the College of Philosophy at the University of Bologna, published a treatise in 1625 called *Trattato come de una lettera missiva si conoscano la natura, e qualità dello scrittore (How from a Missive Letter One May Know the Nature and Qualities of Its Writer)*, which explored the relationship between handwriting and personality.

Two hundred years later in Paris, the priest and scholar Abbé Flandrin (1804–1864) and his student Abbé Jean-Hippolyte Michon (1806–1881) devoted much of their lives to the study of handwriting. Michon subsequently published papers on his system of handwriting analysis, which detailed how specific elements or "signs" (such as strokes and individual letterforms) correspond to particular personality traits. He coined the name *graphology* to describe this study. This term and his method became widely known and accepted. Michon is also credited with stimulating widespread interest in graphology in both public and academic circles, and he was the founder of the Societé Français de Graphologie, a leading institute that still exists.

Another Frenchman and student of Michon's, Jules Crepieux-Jamin (1858–1940), took his theories one step further. Instead of individual "signs" corresponding to specific personality traits, he believed that handwriting should be examined as a whole and that its interpretation should be dependent on other features. He divided the basic elements of handwriting into seven categories: dimension, form, pressure, speed, direction, layout, and continuity. Crepieux-Jamin's approach became the basis of the French school of graphology. It also became influential in the field of psychology and laid the groundwork for the Gestalt approach to handwriting analysis.

Toward the end of the nineteenth century, the Germans jumped on the graphology bandwagon and began making their own contributions to the field. Wilhelm Preyer (1841–1897), a professor of physiology, compared the handwriting of individuals when, the hand, the foot, and even the mouth held the pen. Preyer noted marked similarities in the form and structure of each sample and concluded that "hand" writing is really "brain" writing, because it is centrally organized in the brain. The process of mentally or physically visualizing letters and then transmitting that information to the sensory and motor areas in the brain that control our motor skills is what creates our writing form on paper. This insight has been confirmed by our knowledge that people who have had a stroke see their handwriting as seriously impaired, whereas those who have a hand prosthesis can eventually recover their handwriting skills. Another German psychiatrist, George Meyer, discovered that moods and emotions account for subtle changes in handwriting. These revelations of Preyer and Meyer inspired other psychologists and scientists to become interested in graphology.

Around the turn of the twentieth century, Ludwig Klages (1872–1956), a philosopher and graphologist, and author of *Die Handschrift als Gehernschrift,* applied Gestalt theory (*Gestalt* meaning "complete" or "whole") to his studies, broadening the scope of graphology. He is thus responsible for founding the German school of graphology, which looks at the whole of a handwriting sample rather than equating an individual stroke with a particular trait. Klages also introduced students of graphology to the concept of *rhythm* in writing (i.e., the ease with which the writer expresses the contraction and release in the writing pattern and stroke on the page—whether it is stilted or spontaneous, and shows fluidity in the implementation of the letters). Klages coined the phrase "form level," which refers to the overall pattern of the writing by its style, symmetry, simplicity, legibility, creativity, good movement, and rhythm. He also concluded that handwriting is a balance between the conscious and unconscious aspects of our nature. This view could be compared to music in terms of rhythm, harmony, and psychic balance.

In Switzerland, Max Pulver (1890–1953), a professor at the University of Zurich, studied Klages's work and applied the psychological methods of Carl Jung and Sigmund Freud to handwriting analysis. He classified handwriting into three "zones"—upper, middle, and lower—each corresponding with a distinct area of personality (similar to Freud's discovery of the superego, ego, and id). Pulver also introduced the symbolism of the space on the page—the meaning of the left and right sides of the page, as well as what the width or narrowness of the top, bottom, and side margins means.

* * *

DID YOU KNOW?

Famous people who were fascinated by the hidden language of handwriting include Shakespeare, Charles Dickens, Edgar Allan Poe, Elizabeth Barrett Browning, Carl Jung, and Albert Einstein. They made accurate observations about people in relation to their handwriting.

* * *

Other contributions in graphology were made by Robert Saudek (1880–1935), a Czechoslovakian who conducted experiments on the speed of handwriting, and Rudolph Pophal (1893–1966), a professor of neurology in Hamburg, Germany, who studied how the brain affects written strokes on a page and introduced the concept of tension and release in handwriting. As a neurologist, Pophal studied brain functions and conducted research on the physiological side of handwriting and behavior, confirming once again that writing comes not from our hand but from impulses in our brain.

Edgar Berillon (1859–1948), a French psychologist and an authority on mental illness, found that written exercises could alter behavior in patients, thereby noting the relationship between the mind and writing. He called his study "psychothérapie graphique," which eventually led to the study and practice of graphotherapy. Pierre Janet (1859–1947), a highly respected French psychologist who conducted many studies on the unconscious mind, became interested in and subsequently validated Berillon's findings. This work led to further studies and testing at the Sorbonne. In the 1950s, hundreds of mentally disturbed children were treated through graphotherapy. And in 1966 Paul de Sainte Colombe (1891–1972) published *Grapho-Therapeutics.*

Klara Roman (1881–1962), a brilliant practitioner from Hungary, studied the conscious and unconscious energy of personality as depicted in handwriting, as well as the relationship between speech and handwriting. Roman devised the Psychogram, a measurement tool that compares writing with the character of the writer. She also brought graphology to the United States through classes at the New School in New York City.

Roda Wieser, a German graphologist, studied the handwriting of criminals and discovered basic rhythms that can show criminal tendencies, in particular, the slackness and the rigidity of the stroke.

Graphology didn't make its way across the Atlantic until the early twentieth century. Many noted European graphologists, particularly those native to Germany, Austria, and Eastern Europe, immigrated to the United States and Israel during World War II, when the Nazis were in power. Their knowledge and contributions fueled interest in graphology on both continents.

In 1929 Milton Bunker (1892–1961), a former shorthand teacher from Kansas, founded the International Graphoanalysis Society (IGAS). He developed and standardized a system of handwriting analysis known as Graphoanalysis, which identifies basic handwriting strokes and relates them to particular personality traits (similar to the method developed by Michon a century earlier).

In New York, Felix Klein (1911–1994) founded the National Society for Graphology in 1972. His methods model the German Gestalt, or holistic approach to analysis, emphasizing the psychological interpretation of handwriting. Gestalt graphology requires years of rigorous training and is distinguished from other types of graphology because it takes a global view of handwriting rather than a letter-by-letter analysis. As an internationally respected leader of the Gestalt school, Felix Klein became interested in graphology at the age of thirteen. When later he and his siblings were interned in a concentration camp, Klein became fascinated by the similarities in the pen strokes he noticed among his fellow prisoners. The camp experience formed the basis of his work on the effects of trauma in handwriting, which he referred to as "displaced pressure." This indicates the bending of the spine, or downstroke, in certain letters, revealing the writer's anxiety over the past or the future. (When these prisoners were released and integrated successfully into the community, the spines of their letters subsequently returned to their previous form.)

Alfred Binet (1857–1911), the psychologist who developed the IQ (intelligence quotient) test, supported the findings of graphology and confirmed that certain character traits are reflected in handwriting.

Thea Stein Lewinson (1907–2000) in collaboration with Joseph Zubin (1900–1990) took a decisive step toward a more objective method of graphology in 1942. Zubin, a statistician and medical doctor at Bellevue Hospital in New York, tested the hypothesis of "finding a common denominator for evaluating the qualitative and quantitative aspects of handwriting." Although it was based on the work of Ludwig Klages, this method goes on to investigate the vertical and horizontal movement in writing. The balanced handwriting movement lies between contraction and release.

Lewinson and Zubin then developed a system of scales, which they applied clinically to the handwriting of normal and abnormal individuals. Their painstaking efforts resulted in the establishment of ratings and measurements. After participating in the Lewinson-Zubin experiment, Rose Wolfson published her study of the handwriting of delinquents and nondelinquents. By analyzing twenty-two factors reflected in four lines of writing samples, she found significant differences between the two groups. Lewinson, Zubin, and Wolfson developed a scale determining a writer's emotional control by means of geometric measurements and qualitative ratings.

*   *   *

Did You Know?

Albert Einstein wrote to Thea Stein Lewinson expressing his regard and fascination for the discipline of graphology, saying her analysis of the character of Adolf Hitler was far more revealing and insightful than his own perceptions.

*   *   *

Now in the twenty-first century, more and more businesses and individuals in the United States and other countries are realizing the benefits of using handwriting analysis, and the field continues to grow.

Art, Science, or New Age?

Many consider graphology both an art and a science. Interpreting the variables—separately and in totality—that constitute a handwriting's style is an art. The skill and knowledge of the range of styles factor into that art as well. As a science, graphology measures numerous aspects of handwriting, then notes the similarities between the personalities of writers who share these traits. Over the last two hundred years, graphologists have diligently collected samples to back up their conclusions.

Eighty-nine percent of Swiss companies[1] (compared to 67 percent that use psychological testing) and about 85 percent of French firms[2] use graphology in making personnel decisions.

---

1. International Graphology Conference, University of Zuirich, October 1998.
2. The *Wall Street Journal,* September 3, 1988.

Graphology is an old, well-studied, and well-applied projective psychological approach to the study of personality. It was used before psychoanalysis, Gestalt therapy, and other methods were developed and honed. But somehow, in the United States, graphology is still often categorized as an occult or New Age subject.

While astrology, numerology, and other New Age practices are used to assess the nature and personality of the individual, and are often billed as tools for predicting the future, graphology is *not* a divination tool. It is grounded in psychology, and in fact has been taught in departments of psychology at universities in Germany, France, Spain, Israel, and Italy. The purpose of graphology is to examine and evaluate personality and character. Its use is comparable to assessment models such as the Myers-Briggs Type Indicator (which is widely employed in business), or other psychological testing models. And while handwriting can provide insight into the writer's past and current state of mind, abilities, and compatibility with others, it cannot predict when he or she will meet a soul mate, accumulate wealth, or find peace and happiness.

As a method of personality assessment, handwriting analysis has been validated by centuries of research from major universities and independent studies worldwide. Though graphology is sure to meet its share of skeptics, its use has been taken seriously years by many scientists and psychologists, and, most important, by some of the largest and most renowned corporations and government agencies in the world, such as the Warburg Bank in London, General Motors, Renault, the FBI, the CIA, the Israeli Secret Service (Mossad), and Scotland Yard. In 1980 the Library of Congress changed the classification for graphology books from the "occult" section to the "psychology" section, officially moving graphology out of the New Age.

Graphology Today: Its Uses and Applications

In the early part of the twentieth century, graphology was seriously studied, applied, and practiced throughout Europe. Graphology declined in use in Germany and Nazi-occupied countries during World War II (which is why many of the most renowned graphologists of the time fled to other parts of Europe, Israel, or the United States), but graphology has since steadily grown in popularity and use. Graphological societies and organizations exist in the United States, England, France, Switzerland, Spain, the Netherlands, Scandinavia, Italy, Israel, Singapore, Japan, China, Australia, and New Zealand, and since the fall of the Berlin Wall and the breakup of the Soviet Union, they are returning to Eastern Europe. Classes in graphology are taught in universities.

Graphology is used today in numerous areas, including education, guidance or vocational counseling, profiling job applicants, career assessment, business motivation, analysis of business and personal relationship compatibility, and screening of prospective jurors.

*   *   *

DID YOU KNOW?

Ruth Holmes, a noted graphologist, was hired by Dr. Jack Kervorkian's counsel to aid in jury selection during his assisted suicide trials. Her work proved quite successful.

*   *   *

An in-depth analysis of handwriting can shed new light on a person's values, beliefs, character traits, talents, and abilities. It can provide an accurate picture of the personality in general. It cannot, however, reveal the writer's age, gender, race, religion, handedness, or ethnicity. Since it is nondiscriminatory, graphology is one of many excellent human resources tools. In fact, graphologists working for personnel departments rarely meet the employment candidates—they make their observations on handwriting alone.

The Signature: Power and Identity

The pen is mightier than the sword.

—EDWARD GEORGE BULWER-LYTTON

Handwriting is a very individual trademark. Since no two people have the same handwriting, signatures have been legally binding on documents of all types: contracts, wills, checks, and the Declaration of Independence, to name a few (the signature is often referred to as a "John Hancock," since his handwriting was so prominent on this historic document!). Your signature is your personal seal. And if someone tries to reproduce it, that's forgery, which is considered a crime. Sir William Herschel, who developed the system of fingerprint identification, confirmed the uniqueness of one's signature; he believed that handwriting reveals character in the same way that a fingerprint reveals identity.

Handwriting is special and sometimes even coveted. Think of how valuable autographs are. Collecting autographs is a serious hobby to many people, whether for long-term profit or simply for the fun and excitement of having the signature of someone you admire or respect.

Can a signature alone give a glimpse into someone's character? To a degree. Of course, it is always preferable to have a *page* of writing to analyze—a signature might be different from the text of a handwriting, and the longer or more varied a sample you have, the better and more accurate your view of that person and his or her character. However, interesting character revelations can often be derived from how one's name is signed. We'll look at some famous—and infamous—signatures later in this book, with the proviso that a signature represents a *very limited* sample of writing. Still, because it is the most practiced writing we create, our signature is considered our psychological calling card.

* * *

Did You Know?

January 12 is National Handwriting Day and January 6 through 12 is National Handwriting Analysis Week (sponsored by the American Association of Handwriting Analysts and the American Handwriting Analysis Foundation). Celebrate it write!

* * *

Handwriting in the Computer Age

In our current information age, more and more people are using computers to communicate. Instead of writing in longhand, we're typing out our term papers, business reports, or novels using word-processing programs on computers. Instead of drafting handwritten letters to friends in other cities and countries, we now use e-mail. While all this makes communication faster and life a lot easier, it means there's a lot less old-fashioned writing going on. And e-mail is not a living expression of the writer, nor does it become a keepsake of the author.

Some computer programs will create a font that replicates your handwriting or signature. You've probably even noticed that your paycheck now has a computer-generated signature rather than the real thing. If you've ever used a personal digital assistant (like the Palm Pilot or Clié), you've probably seen the software called Graffiti, which turns your handwritten strokes into letters (albeit not always as accurately as you'd like). And the Tablet PC is a developing technology in which a digital pen can be used on a tablet or screen to turn your written words into printed language on the computer. Microsoft's CEO, Bill Gates, believes that the Tablet PC "will be the most popular form of PC sold in America."

There are also computer programs that claim to analyze your handwriting in moments. Though some programs can help the professional graphologist expedite the input and output of information, the student of graphology or layperson wanting to understand how to read handwriting would best do it the old-fashioned way—by reading books written by serious professionals, taking classes, and collecting and studying actual handwriting samples. The more you study and interpret, the better at it you will become.

Without real handwriting and a knowledgeable professional doing the analysis, there is no accounting for accuracy.

It is widely believed that no computer program existing today can consistently pick up all the nuances in a handwriting sample, or provide the personal insights and reliable instincts of a trained professional. Would you want your doctor to make a diagnosis about an illness based purely on your filling out a questionnaire, without the benefit of an in-person examination?

Nothing will ever take the place of the intimacy that a personal, handwritten note or signature delivers. Imagine getting a romantic love letter printed in Times Roman. Or not signing your five-year-old's birthday card, "Love, Mom" or "Love, Dad." There will always be times when writing by hand will be appropriate or simpler. As we forge into the future, our identities might become as impersonal as keypunches in a giant data bank, but our signatures will still be uniquely *our own*.

CHAPTER 2

Different Strokes for Different Folks

❧   ❧   ❧

UNDERSTANDING WRITING STYLES AND TECHNIQUES

Each handwriting is as unique as a thumbprint.
It is an outward reflection of one's inner character.
There are many attributes to consider when analyzing
a handwriting sample: margins, spacing, zones, size,
connectivity, strokes, slants, movement, rhythm,
regularity, speed, and pressure. Each of these
will be outlined and described
in this chapter.

THE SAYING "MIND YOUR P'S AND Q'S" has a far different meaning to a professional graphologist than it might to the rest of us. After reading just a few lines of a person's handwriting, a skilled graphologist can form a very clear picture of the writer's personality, strengths, and weaknesses.

How can you use that same source of information to better understand what makes the people in your life tick? Well, you can start by familiarizing yourself with the various handwriting elements. These include the margins, spacing, size and form of letters, how the letters connect, slant, movement, speed, the pressure of the stroke on the page, and more. Knowledge of these elements and what they say about character will help you build accurate "personality profiles" of the people with whom you come in contact. The more you understand the people in your life, the better you'll know how to relate to them!

Let's take a closer look at the factors that make up the whole pattern of a handwriting and what each of these factors tells us about the writer.

How It Looks on a Page

All writing starts with a blank page. Ten people can each be given a blank sheet of paper to write on, and each person will fill that page with writing in a different way.

We consciously try to keep our handwriting consistent in the first line or two. But as our thoughts about *what* we're writing become more important than *how* we're writing, our writing pattern becomes a lot more unconscious and revealing. Thus, the way we—or any writer—use space on a page allows initial insight into character, habits, and life patterns. In general, the overall form or pattern of the margins, lines, and words on a page reveals the writer's capacity to channel energy into goals.

Margins

A margin is the perimeter that frames a page of writing. When you type a document on a computer, your word-processing program opens with preset margins that are usually at least one inch all around, so that your document looks symmetrical on a page and has enough border to be easy on the eyes. But when you write a letter, essay, or report *by hand,* you don't possess that computer-like precision; the placement of your words on the page is uniquely yours and an innate reflection of who you are and where you are going.

*   *   *

Did You Know?

Studies have proven that if you write in the dark, you cannot keep a consistent margin!

*   *   *

Let's take a look at the types of margins and what they say about the personality of the writer.

Margins Around Page

Depending on the amount of space allotted to the margins around a page (both width and length), it could indicate either options available or a sense of aesthetics.

Balanced Margins Around Page

This is a sample of my current handwriting - and even though you have requested that writing

Qualities

- A good planner
- Neat, orderly, and organized
- Well adjusted to the world

Narrow Margins All Around Page

> It helps you to begin to
> understand why you prefer
> certain methods, styles, ways
> to use graphology. It opens up
> some valuable insights |...&

Qualities

- Doesn't give space to others
- Multitasker
- Often shows lower level of education
- Problem with ego boundaries, i.e., defining a clear relationship with others

Wide Margins All Around

> Dear Roger,
>
> I would really love to go back to Greece
> I think it is one of the most beautiful places
> to visit.

Qualities

- Protective of self
- Shies away from physical contact
- Needs privacy

The Left Margin

The left margin is indicative of the appearance you want to make to others. It also expresses your feelings about the past, your mother, and your degree of formality.

Consistently Narrow Left Margin

Qualities

- Likes familiarity
- Casual and informal
- Reduced respect for education
- Careful with money

Narrowing Left Margin

Qualities

- Cautious
- Protective
- May lose enthusiasm for things after starting them

Consistently Wide Left Margin

The packet of samples enclosed is for your amusement/edification or whatever. Today the pressure is really on: money works wonders — gotta find a way to make some!

Qualities

- High standards
- Running from the past
- Open to opportunity
- Reserved, self-control
- Possesses self-respect

Widening Left Margin

As troubles seem to continue to assail us from every part of the world, may I pray that in the new millennium we may hope for a more peaceful solution may

Qualities

- Enthusiastic about reaching goals
- Impatient and hasty
- Extravagant
- Less trusting of others

Straight Left Margin

> True excellence requires a worthy dream, a good idea of how to realize it, and the The courage to risk failure to achieve it.

Quality

• Respect for learning, education, culture

The Right Margin

The right margin reflects how you face the future and your need to reach your goals and objectives. Right margins don't come under the same scrutiny as left margins because it is perfectly normal for a right margin to be somewhat irregular. If a writer does have a perfectly aligned right margin, watch out! This is a person who may have some real emotional issues!

The right margin also reflects your feelings and attitudes toward your father.

Consistently Wide Right Margin

Qualities

- Cautious
- Fearful of the future
- Anxious
- Oversensitive

Widening Right Margin

Qualities

- Shy
- Needs a lot of encouragement
- Fearful and mistrustful of others

Consistently Narrow Right Margin

> *Well. I've been putting this off for a long time now! I think I'm ready to hear what you have to say about me. I met this man in August of*

Qualities

- Active
- Goal- and future-oriented
- Vital and outgoing, engages people
- Hasty

Inconsistent Right Margin

> *Listen, Learn, Help, Lead are the Keys to excellence in leadership.*
> *You have to learn everyday and set high*

Qualities

- Tendency toward moodiness
- Uncertainty about goals
- Ambivalence about the future

Narrowing Right Margin

Qualities

- Loves a challenge
- Eagerness
- Takes risks

Straight Right Margin

Qualities

- Exhibits self-control
- Slow to adapt
- Consistent regarding goals

The Upper Margin

The upper margin indicates your respect and deference for the reader and your sense of protocol.

Narrow Upper Margin

Qualities

- Informal
- Inconsiderate
- Possibly lacking respect

Wide Upper Margin

Qualities

- Modest
- Reserved
- Respectful

The Lower Margin

The lower margin reflects your personal enthusiasm (or lack thereof).

Narrow Lower Margin

If I'm in a house & can find clean sheets, a towel, & a pillow, you're invited to spend the night ~ & if we can catch you coming & going — I'll just leave the sheets on! Obviously, I'll be in Charlottesville trying to arrange for housing during this pd., too — So — what I'm saying is ~ my schedule is crazy at this time — if at all possible, tho' ~ we want to connect with you if it fits into your plans, too.

Qualities

- Dreamer
- Sentimental
- Economical

Wide Lower Margin

Qualities

- Superficial
- Aloof
- Emotional or sexual issues

Crowded Writing at End of Page

If writing is squeezed into the bottom of the page, it may also mean there is an inability to plan or anticipate well.

Spacing

After margins, there are three more spatial factors to consider: the space between the lines, the space between the words, and the space between letters in a word.

Line Spacing

The space between lines of writing generally indicates planning and goal setting, organizational abilities, self-control, logic, and emotional clarity.

Balanced Line Spacing

> Do what you can to show
> you care about other people,
> and you will make our
> world a better place.
>   Rosalynn Carter

Qualities

- Mental clarity
- Organized
- Good planning skills
- Objective
- Common sense

Narrow Line Spacing

> Divorce situation still unresolved (she will r
> Just took "the Totem" (I had ESP a 50).. her now seminar
> peace + love

Qualities

- Lack of reserve
- Lack of self-knowledge
- Thrifty
- Unclear judgment

Overlapping Lines

Qualities

- Lack of inhibitions
- Lack of perspective
- Chaotic and disorganized thinking
- Lack of consideration for others

Wide Line Spacing

Qualities

- Analytical mind
- Well organized
- Good manners
- Elegant and refined
- Detached, clear judgment
- Anxiety
- Emotional isolation

Irregular Line Spacing

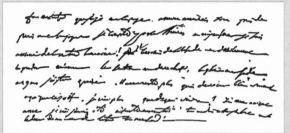

Qualities

- Lacks self-discipline and self-confidence
- Reacts to the moment
- Impulsive, mood swings

Word Spacing

Spacing between words tells us much about your personal space in regard to other people—are you easygoing or a little restrained? It also reflects your speech patterns—if a writer pauses to breathe or speeds up when talking, the flow of his or her words on paper will often mirror that individual's speech.

Balanced Word Spacing

Qualities

- Well balanced
- Mindful of boundaries (hers and others)

Narrow Word Spacing

Qualities

- Talkative
- Self-confident
- Active
- Demonstrative with others
- Outgoing
- Careful with money

Very Narrow Word Spacing

Qualities

- Boundary issues
- Impulsive
- Dependent on others

(Clinging to the baseline is another indicator of these traits.)

Wide Word Spacing

[handwriting sample]

Qualities

- Selective in relationships
- Reserved and a bit standoffish
- Poetic and/or philosophical
- Good listener

Very Wide Word Spacing

[handwriting sample]

Qualities

- Shy or hesitant
- Fearful of intimacy; inhibited
- Isolated and lonely

Irregular Word Spacing

Qualities

- Emotionally unstable
- Conflicted and unpredictable
- Impatient

- Unreliable
- Lacks a clear sense of boundaries in relation to self and others

Letter Spacing

The spaces between letters within a word are indicative of self-expression and, in relationships, warmth and openness. The closer the letters, the more inhibited the person; the wider apart the letters, the more open and giving the person.

Balanced Letter Spacing

Qualities

- Adaptable
- Warm and friendly

- Open-minded

Narrow Letter Spacing

Teaching sometimes drains
me of energy and patience

Qualities

- Refusal to reflect or practice introspection on oneself and life in general

Wide Letter Spacing

The enclosed is
self-explanatory-

Qualities

- Outgoing
- Chatty
- Spontaneous

Space After First Letter

Qualities

- Cautious
- Gets the "lay of the land" before taking action

Irregular Letter Spacing

Quality

- Ambivalent

Getting in "The Zone"

As your pen moves horizontally across the page, the letters you form also move vertically through each of the three zones, which correspond to both your psyche and your body. Each zone embraces a specific sphere of life: mind, body, and spirit, or as Freud would say, the ego, the id, and the superego.

Let's start with the basics—or, rather, the baseline.

The Baseline

The baseline is the line—the "horizon" or ground—on which handwriting rests. It can be visible, for example when you're writing on ruled paper, or "invisible," as when you're writing on unlined paper. The baseline separates the conscious from the unconscious. It indicates emotional stability, realism, balance, and ability to set goals.

The closer and more consistently writing rests on the baseline, the more stable a personality the writer is likely to have. When the writing strays above the baseline, it reflects an adventurous personality—someone who is not tied to conventions or rules, who prefers to go her own way. When handwriting falls below the baseline, it indicates emotional heaviness, reduced enthusiasm, depressed moods, inappropriateness, and appreciation of money and material things.

A steady and straight baseline reveals a goal-oriented individual. A wavy baseline shows someone who's more interested in the journey than in the destination. Beware: An overly wavy baseline expresses a personality that can be unstable and capable of many moods.

Steady Baseline

Wavy Baseline

The baseline is also the point from which we can begin to examine the three writing zones.

Zoning In on the Zones

How do you spot a zone? Letters that fall on the baseline (all of the vowels, plus *c, m, n, r, s, v, w,* and *x*) are in the middle zone; letters that extend high above the baseline (*b, d, f, h, k, l,* and *t*), are in the upper zone; and letters that extend below the baseline (*f, g, j, p, q, y,* and *z*) represent the lower zone.

Each zone reflects a different level of consciousness and personality manifestation. To use a metaphor, the upper zone can represent the sky, which reflects our aspirations, creative fantasies, and goals not yet achieved. The middle zone is the horizon—the place on which we rest our feet—our daily existence. The lower zone represents that which is hidden and unconscious but influences us nonetheless. Although we are often unaware of its influence, our unconscious has a powerful impact on our upper and middle zones. Its emphasis, intensity, or prominence in the handwriting reflects the value the writer places on each zone.

The Upper Zone

The upper portions of tall and capital letters, i-dots, and t-bars, usually fall into the upper zone above the small letters. This zone is also where we see the stems and loops of the letters *b, d, f, h, k, l,* and *t.* This zone—and the emphasis given it by the shapes and sizes of the upper loops the writer makes—represents the writer's relationship with authority, father, fantasies, dreams, aspirations, ambitions, concepts, and speculation. This zone deals with intuition, imagination, and sphere of abstraction. Freud would say this represents the *superego*—rules, regulations, and the standards and ideals to which one is supposed to aspire.

The upper zone also gives clues to the writer's intellect, interests, and spiritual development.

My personal definition of success is - "peace of mind which is a direct result of self-satisfaction in knowing you made the effort to become the best of which you are capable."

If there is emphasis on the upper zone, it usually indicates that there's an issue with the ego, i.e., the need to compensate for ego insecurities and pride. Wide loops in the upper zone reflect an active imagination and mean that the writer might show unrealistic expectations and grandiosity. If a writer has a short upper zone, it usually means that he has issues with authority figures and tends to favor the concrete over the abstract.

Exaggerated Upper Zone

Yours sincerely,

Ivan F. Boesky
Managing Partner

Short Upper Zone

PEN POINT Capital Letters

Capital or uppercase letters reveal the way one wishes to be viewed by others. If the capital letter is large, followed by small middle zone writing, it shows that the person wishes to present himself as confident but in reality does not feel nearly so secure. Capital letters that are highly embellished or oversized can indicate vanity and artifice, as well as pretense and a desire to overcompensate. Small capital letters reflect modesty or lack of pretension. (See sample of Ivan Boesky on page 38.)

Capital *I*

In the English language, the capital *I* is unique. It is not just a letter but also a word—a personal pronoun that represents both one's self-concept and one's parents. The capital *I* represents not only the writer but also feelings about self-worth and how one wishes to be regarded by others.

The Middle Zone

The middle zone is where 90 percent of all writing takes place. Small letters fall within the middle zone, where they are connected on the baseline. These letters are *a, c, e, i, m, n, o, r, s, u, v, w*, and *x*, and they do not extend to the upper zone or the lower zone. This zone represents the way one adapts to reality, copes with everyday life, and the expression of the ego. This is also the zone of connection with others, as well as of feeling and emotion. It reveals the writer's sense of "relatedness."

Look forward to seeing you in Ann Arbor.

If the middle zone is in a harmonious proportion to the rest of the writing pattern, the writer is a relatively well-integrated individual who has made a good adjustment to life. Large middle zone writing shows self-involvement and, to some extent, narcissism. A small middle zone can indicate that the writer tends to underrate his or her gifts and may feel inferior.

The Lower Zone

The letters extending below the baseline belong to the lower zone. These include the letters *f, g, j, p, q, y,* and *z.* The lower zone is a deeply personal area, focusing on the writer's material needs, primal instincts, creative drive, and search for answers to life's perplexing questions. It can also reveal hidden aggression.

Average Lower Zone

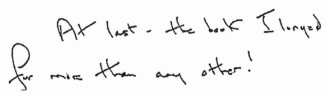

This zone represents the unconscious as well. An accented lower zone represents a strong search for fulfillment and material rewards. It also indicates sexuality, personal needs, and a search for roots. The lower zone represents the traits most often hidden from others, or what Freud would call the *id.* While the middle zone represents the conscious, the lower zone represents that which is below our threshold of consciousness and can also reveal a person's dark side.

If the lower zone is inflated and the middle zone small, it can mean that areas of energy—such as fantasies or frustrations—are not adequately channeled into reality.

Inflated Upper Zone

* * *

DID YOU KNOW?

The lowercase *f* is the only letter that extends into all three zones.

* * *

Size Matters

In writing, size does matter! The pattern of the writing and the way it is spread over the page represent how much emotional and physical space the writer demands. The height shows the need for recognition and aspirations, and the horizontal expansion shows the need for self-expression. Small handwriting indicates someone who is not concerned with what others think and one who can work alone in highly detailed, often demanding fields in which she can play a contributing role. This is in no way, however, an indication of strength and self-worth.

What's Average?

How do you gauge what's big and what's small? Start at the middle! In general, a handwriting is considered average size when letters in the middle zone measure about 3 millimeters high, the upper zone letters measure 6 millimeters from the baseline to the top of the loop, and the lower zone letters measure about 6 millimeters from baseline to the bottom of the loop.

This is a sample of average-sized writing.
Notice how the letters are well proportioned.

Medium Size Writing

Writing that is medium or average size is the norm for most people, but size can change with age, moods, stress, illness, or medication.

Average Writing

As a result, I would like to call a group meeting to discuss this issue. Can you be available to meet on Wednesday at 11 AM?

Qualities

- Focused
- Well adjusted
- Good social skills
- Realistic
- Plays by the rules

Large Writing

the veiws demonstrated herein are not necessarily the veiws of the management, but consist mainly of a personal nature.

Qualities

- Enthusiastic
- Extravagant
- Proud
- Entrepreneurial
- Bold
- Independent
- Action-oriented
- Needing attention

Small Legible Writing

[handwriting sample]

> your pictures are faster than
> mine! Thanks so much for
> the print. It was really colorful.
> As you have noticed by now, I
> have some for you too. I like
> the one of you with Buddha very

Qualities

- Pragmatic
- Modest
- Dutiful
- Objective
- Good concentration and focus

Uneven Writing Size

[handwriting sample]

> and then we went to

Qualities

- Varying responses to situations
- Uneven self-esteem
- Over- or underestimation of self-worth

How Do You Connect?

When we write in script, words are formed by joining one letter to another. We further join them by making an upstroke or a downstroke. The point at which we join each letter to another is called a *connection,* and the style with which we make those connections is called *connective form.* The connective form reveals a lot about emotions, energy, and flexibility.

Handwriting is primarily made up of four connective forms: the garland, arcade, angle, and thread, and sometimes a combination of forms.

The Garland

The garland is the most common form of the writing connectors and also the easiest to create. The garland's *u* form resembles an open cup and has a lovely, fluid rhythm. The way to recognize the garland, particularly in the *m* and the *n,* is to notice if the letter is curved at the bottom and pointed at the top. And because it represents an open cup, the garland allows stimuli to enter from the outside and, in particular, from the upper zone, representing the intellect. But it closes out stimulation from the lower zone, which means that the writer is open to his emotional, creative, and intellectual level. The garland form indicates a person who is adaptable, tolerant, straightforward, and good-natured. This is a person who is open to outside influences, likes nature, and can be a good mediator in conflict resolution.

A *strong garland,* which has a wide curve
on the bottom, indicates these qualities:

- Flexible
- Talkative
- Tolerant
- Good-natured

> I shall get into contact with
> you then and am looking

A *weak garland,* which is often narrow
and does not show a strong, regular curve
on the bottom, indicates these qualities:

- Unstable
- Unable to concentrate
- Naïve
- Acquiescent
- Insincere

> We are planning something around
> 14th (Dec.) & will be in touch. Hope

The Arcade

The arcade is the reverse of the garland connection. It resembles a cup turned upside down. The arcade is rounded at the top of the middle zone and angled along the baseline. It is a connective form that is slower in creation and movement. The arcade requires more caution and less spontaneity because you need control to produce it. It shows secretiveness and reserve. Writers of this form are less likely to be influenced by their emotions and more involved with formality, tradition, protocol, and conventions. Often artists, architects, and writers who are concerned with form and structure use this technique of connection.

The Angle

Both the garland and the arcade connections move toward the right of the page, but the angular form is more static and stilted. It takes longer to write in angles than any other connecting form because the pen stops at each intersection. The shape and rhythm of the angle connector are reminiscent of a military march. Angles are harder to create, require more intensity and discipline, and they are more likely to break the natural flow or rhythm of the movement.

Writers who use an angle connection love challenges, have strong willpower, and are not adaptable—they expect *you* to adapt to them! Angles show a need for control of both the self and others. Because they are often intense on the page, producing the most friction, angle connections show the need for conflict—and an opportunity to overcome it.

Donald Trump is an angle writer

The angle form is not open to influences of either the upper or the lower zone, and it is often more contracted than released. Because of an inability to adapt as easily as the garland writer, for example, the angle writer can be uninterested in the needs or feelings of others. Adjustment and flexibility are great challenges to the angle writer.

The Thread

The thread is not really a connector but, in fact, an avoidance of one. The advantage of the thread is that it allows great freedom, spontaneity, and very little need for focus. It permits speed and versatility, and allows the writer to see all sides of a situation before choosing to act. Use of the thread can reflect opportunism, manipulation, and diplomacy. While the writer may appear to obey all the rules, he or she often figures out a way to circumvent them too. Creative people, or people who have very quick minds, love this connection because it doesn't slow them down. However, it can be used for deception, deviousness, ambiguity, lack of commitment, and disloyalty.

The thread signals a person who is a nonconformist and who is capable of dealing with any situation. This shapeless connection allows the writer to operate free from the restrictions that the other forms of connections require. This connection also signifies the writer's need to choose his or her own path. Independence keeps this person happy.

There are two types of threads: *primary* and *secondary*.

The pressure of the pen on the page creates the *primary thread*. The final stroke in a word or sentence thins out but is still legible. This writer can act and think quickly on her feet. She is adaptable and intuitive.

The *secondary thread* is created by pressure of the grip against the nib of the pen on the page, so the handwriting is less legible. This writer can be seen as manipulative, selfish, and a bit of an opportunist. To confirm these qualities, the connection must be evaluated in the context of the total writing pattern.

Henry Kissinger is a thread writer

Different Strokes

The stroke is the path traced by the pen on paper, a visual record of the writing movement. Writing is, in effect, frozen movement on the page. The size, shape, and form of the stroke—the up, down, and across movements—leave their imprint on the page. The imprint reflects the smoothness, fluency, and firmness of the stroke. The hand usually applies more pressure in making the downstroke than in making the upstroke. The fingers are pointing toward the body for the downstroke, whereas they are stretched (involving more strain) for the upstroke. Strokes show us much about the person wielding the instrument. Let's look at the types of strokes that form the written word.

Downstroke

The way the downstroke is made reveals the writer's attitude toward outside forces and values.

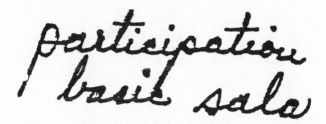

Downstroke from the Upper to the Middle Zone

The writer brings his or her creative fantasies (from the upper zone) into conscious reality (in the middle zone) to make real an abstract idea.

Upstroke from the Middle Zone

The writer consciously wishes to move from today's reality to future aspirations and ambitions.

Upstroke from the Lower Zone

The writer brings instinctive and primal needs and drives into conscious reality.

School Type (or Copybook)

The school type writer needs approval or prefers guidelines in order to fulfill responsibilities. This style may also show an aversion to taking risks. This writer generally is comfortable with the form of writing learned as a student or a schoolteacher—in fact, he or she might *be* a teacher.

Sharp Stroke

The writer values clear boundaries, is focused, articulate, and analytical. If the stroke is weak, the individual may be outwardly cold, easily offended, or lacking in energy.

Pastose Strokes

A pastose stroke is usually written with a felt-tipped pen, which makes it thick and brushlike, with a preference for reduced friction on the page. The writer is warm, natural, and open to the environment, and enjoys sensory pleasures.

Dr. Polo, a Dr. Armaio Navarro, al Dr. Vargas,

Making the Connection

We've learned about connective forms, but now it's time to consider how words and sentences are joined.

Connections are made by writing impulses. Writing patterns mirror speech patterns; some are fast, some are moderate, and others, slow and deliberate. Connections show us how well the writer connects to the outside world in regard to thoughts and impressions, relationships, and social activities.

Moderately Connected

Moderately connected writing joins many letters but there is often a break between first and/or capital letters and syllables. The moderately connected writer has sharp reasoning skills, has thoughts that flow smoothly, is a good problem solver, is adaptable, and interacts well with other people.

Listen, Learn, Help, Lead are the Keys to excellence in leadership.

You have to learn everyday and set high

Highly Connected

Highly connected writing links most letters with occasional pauses after capital letters. The writer who uses a highly connected style has a good mind for trivia, is detail-oriented, organized, tenacious, and consistent. He or she is logical, realistic, and a systematic thinker who can often achieve goals through willpower rather than energy.

Overconnected

Overconnected writing is seamless with no breaks at all. Sometimes such writing is crowded as well. The overconnected writer can be perceived as compulsive, highly focused, literal, and logical, and she or he often sublimates emotions into a sense of willpower in order to accomplish goals.

Disconnected

Disconnected writing almost has the feel of printed writing. Somewhat disconnected writing indicates an idea person with a good analytical mind. The writer can have friends and acquaintances but may not connect to them in a deep or meaningful way.

Very disconnected, almost choppy writing can be the sign of a highly creative or intuitive person but someone who may not always see his or her ideas come to fruition. This writer's not always good at honing ideas to make them work. Furthermore, this personality can be moody and unpredictable, and not always adept at creating and sustaining relationships.

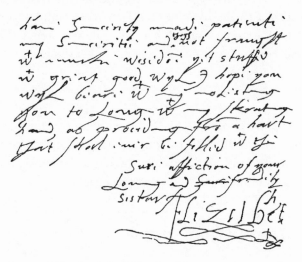

Queen Elizabeth I of England is a good example of disconnected writing

Printing

Believe it or not, printed handwriting *can* be analyzed—it still adheres to many of the forms and styles that apply to script (cursive writing) despite the fact that no individual printed letter will span all three zones.

Though mostly schoolchildren print, there are a variety of times when the average adult needs to print, i.e., when filling out forms and for legibility when writing notes or instructions to others. People who print are often logical and realistic.

With our current emphasis on the computer, cursive writing has begun to take a backseat to printing. Writers who print often do not like their cursive style and feel printing gives them a great sense of control.

With an increasing understanding of the differences between men and women, the quality of relationships and

A New Slant on Slants

The slant of handwriting is the angle formed by strokes going up from or down to the baseline. Slants reflect emotional responses to what is going on in one's life at the time one writes. There are four types of slants: right, upright, left, and variable.

Right Slant

The right slant is an angle of 45 to 85 degrees to the right. It reveals an outward-directed person, focusing on others and on the outside world. It generally means there's an emphasis on taking initiative and on meeting goals and objectives.

Upright Slant

The upright slant is at an angle of 85 to 105 degrees. This vertical writing generally indicates self-reliance and self-discipline. It also reflects poise, discipline, self-control or reserve, introspection, and independence. Writers with an upright or neutral slant are fairly grounded in the present.

Left Slant

The left slant is an angle of 45 to 85 degrees to the left. It reveals an inward-directed person with an emphasis on the self, mother, protection, well-being, safety, and an attachment to the past. It also suggests resistance to change.

This scale offers an easy way to "measure" slants in writing. You can trace and use it whenever you practice an analysis.

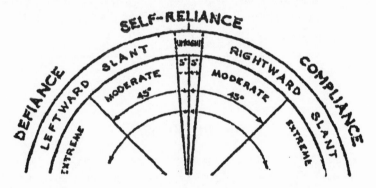

From Klara G. Roman, Handwriting: A Key to Personality

Swinging Both Ways: The Variable Slant

Talk about ambivalence! If you examine a handwriting where the slant changes from right to left to upright to right again (or any combination thereof) you're looking at someone who has real trouble making up his or her mind.

PEN POINT   What About Lefties?

Lefties account for 15 percent of all writers. However, unless writing in Hebrew (which moves from right to left), most left-handed people are confronted with challenges when learning to write. They have to place their paper in odd positions to adapt to the right-handed writing world and avoid having their hands immediately wipe across (and smear) the fresh ink they've written.

As a group, lefties are often considered sensitive, imaginative, and highly creative—Michelangelo, Leonardo da Vinci, and Benjamin Franklin were all left-handed.

In general, left-handed writing is not obvious. Some lefties tend to have more upright and angular handwriting than right-handed writers.

*   *   *

Did You Know?

People whose handwriting slants to the left can often find relationships challenging or difficult. They can also rebel against authority.

*   *   *

Smooth Moves: Writing in Motion

Movement is part and parcel of writing. Once you start writing, your writing moves, and the ways in which it moves—trend, rhythm, speed, spacing, and direction—are important personality indicators.

How Trendy Are You? Right and Left Trends

The Swiss psychologist Max Pulver taught us that the right represents the future and the left, the past. Any horizontal movement toward the left side of the page is called *left trend;* any movement toward the right side of the page is called *right trend.*

What do we mean by *movement?* Right trend movement entails elements such as a rightward slant, letter loops that pull to the right, crossing *t*'s and dotting *i*'s on the right, long ending strokes, and margins that move to the right side of the page. Left trend movement entails elements such as a leftward slant, letter loops that pull to the left, crossing *t*'s and dotting *i*'s, and long beginning strokes.

Right Trend and Left Trend

A left trend represents an emphasis on oneself, withdrawal from others, yearning for influence, and resistance to authority. A general left trend indicates a need for the support of the mother and the past, while a general right trend represents adventure, challenge, the values of the father, and the future.

I've Got Rhythm

The rhythm in handwriting reflects the writer's impulses—the unique contraction and release pattern. Movement, form, and space all work together, to create a rhythm pattern in writing.

Strong Rhythm

> The rain just can't get me down —
> I feel so good. The weekend is like
> a dream now, vivid in my mind's eye
> and oh so special. I love you! The

Qualities

- Self-control
- Stability
- Steadfastness
- Discipline

Weak Rhythm

> Cosell & the Eleventh House,
> fresh from a cold-out
> weekend at Max's positively
> bowled over the audience.
> It obvious that Cosell

Qualities

- Disorganization
- Fickleness
- Changeability
- Lack of self-control
- Nonconformity

Regular Guys—and Gals!

Having perfect regularity (i.e., consistency) in an overall hand-writing style is impossible, but there are general consistencies that indicate regularity.

Regularity

Regularity is demonstrated by maintaining consistent slant, pressure, and height in letters. There is also a consistent return of strokes to the baseline. These characteristics indicate that the writer is stable, disciplined, and able to control impulses. He or she also has a strong sense of duty, reliability, concentration, and willpower.

I'm very interested in how you addressed the contents of the

Irregularity

Fluctuation in slant, pressure, and height in letters shows irregularity, indicating that the writer is apt to have little control over impulses—at times exhibiting rebellious, undisciplined, or careless behavior.

iuq responsibility for eso Uzi $750 I would.

Regularity Versus Rhythm

What's the difference between regularity and rhythm? you ask. According to Felix Klein, the constancy of size, width, pressure, and straightness of lines characterizes regularity. Both regularity and rhythm are reflections of movement. It is the elastic "to-and-fro" movement of the writing—the interchange of movement release and movement contraction—that forms the rhythm. Everyone has individual rhythm.

Faster Than the Speed of Write

Writing speed is an important feature, but it's also one of the most difficult elements to assess accurately. Unless you observe a writer in action, there's no immediate way to know how much time she or he took to write! And the fact that speed can vary from document to document—or even within the same document—poses another challenge. The pace used to take notes during a lecture will likely be different from the pace used to write up a thoughtful letter to a boyfriend or girlfriend. Because you probably won't have more than one handwriting sample from any individual, you won't have the ability to make comparisons and draw a well-rounded conclusion.

Speed in handwriting is a characteristic of great interest to professional graphologists. As noted in Chapter 1, Robert Saudek studied speed, and many graphologists believe it is a crucial element because so many other characteristics are affected by how fast or slow the writing is (and vice versa).

Here are some guidelines for distinguishing slow and fast writing:

S-L-O-W Writing

Basic Elements of Slow Writing

- Disconnected writing
- Angular or arcade connective forms

- Heavy pressure on the page
- Elaborate or decorative writing style
- Regularity
- Upright or left slant and left trend
- Descending baseline
- Narrowing left margin

Common Personality Traits of Slow Writers

- Lacking spontaneity
- Inhibited
- Liking familiarity
- Deliberate
- Formal and reserved
- Contemplative
- Accurate and thorough

FAST Writing

Basic Elements of Fast Writing

- Use of garland or thread connective forms
- Light pressure on the page with a thin stroke
- Irregularity
- Right slant and right trend
- Ascending baseline
- Widening left margin

JOHN F. KENNEDY

Common Personality Traits of Fast Writers

- Spontaneous
- Makes the most of time
- Gets things done
- Active
- Mover and shaker
- Quick thinker and learner

Speedy Gonzalez: Too Fast

If a writer's speed is too fast, he or she can be

- impulsive
- impatient
- careless
- superficial
- hasty

As you would suspect, a writer whose speed is moderate and who has a well-paced release of energy is generally stable and takes things in stride.

Putting the Pressure On

Did you ever get a note in which the writing is so dark and deep you can see and feel the imprint with your fingertips on the back of the page? That's an example of heavy writing pressure.

As previously mentioned, pressure is produced by two factors: the pressure against the pen point, which is called *primary pressure*; and the grip the writer has around the pen, which is called *secondary pressure* and is the basis for pastose writing. To check for pressure, turn the paper over and see how much the writing makes indentations on that page.

The writing surface plays a part in pressure, too. If you write on a paper placed on a wooden desk or table, you'll demonstrate less pressure than if that same page was placed on a pad or softer surface.

The Felt-Tipped Pen

Felt-tipped pens (such as the Flair) show virtually no pressure against the page, making handwriting difficult to analyze. The pattern created by a felt-tipped pen is a consistent brushlike stroke.

People who use felt-tipped pens often prefer a thick stroke, which is a sign of sensuality.

PEN POINT   Don't Hold the Pen Against the Writer

Every now and then, you'll get a bum pen that blots ink (think leaky ballpoint) or discharges ink in a way that creates a fat or almost smearing stroke (think fountain pen). These indicators are more reflections of the pen's personality than of the writer's! When examining a handwriting sample, be mindful of this discrepancy—if the ink blots or smears are consistent throughout, it's the fault of the pen, not the writer, and should not be interpreted as a negative character trait.

Color and Discharge of Ink

If the ink is pale, the writer displays weak emotional energy. He may be cold, superficial, or overly sensitive. If the ink is uneven in discharge, her emotional and physical state may be inconsistent.

Normal Pressure

Characteristics to look for: moderate ink color and slight indentation.

Qualities

- Vitality
- Maturity
- Intelligence
- Good willpower

Heavy Pressure

Characteristics to look for: deep ink color and strong indentation on back of page.

Qualities

- Strong drive
- Willfulness and determination
- Desire for control
- Ability to commit to an objective

Very Heavy Pressure

Characteristics to look for: Indentations so deep they almost rip or distort the paper.

Qualities

- Frustration
- Anger
- Ill temper
- Intensity

Light Pressure

Characteristics to look for: light and delicate writing that barely makes an indentation on the back of the page.

All is well with my friend .

Qualities

- Path of least resistance
- Sensitivity
- Delicacy
- Good mental energy
- Lack of stamina

Pressure in Lower Zone Only

I know how proud you all feel on her. With every wish for your own great happiness - believe me Faithfully yours.

Quality

- For many, an emphasis on sexuality and desire.

(The word *Faithfully* is circled for emphasis. The circle is not part of the original sample.)

* * *

DID YOU KNOW?

Extreme unevenness in pressure is often seen in the handwriting of criminals.

* * *

CHAPTER 3

What's Your Sign?

* * *

THE SIX PERSONALITY "TYPES" IN HANDWRITING

*Handwriting styles can be categorized into six types
or personalities: introvert, extrovert, intuitive, sensing,
thinking, and feeling. Each type will be explained, offering
a more holistic approach to interpreting personality in
handwriting. Writing samples from notable
people will be examined.*

THE NOTED SWISS PSYCHOLOGIST Carl Jung believed that personality can be classified into psychological "types." His theory was based on how average people acquire and expend their energy; how they receive, perceive, absorb, and process information; and how they use that information to make decisions. In his book *Psychological Types,* Jung elaborated on three sets of types, each set consisting of a pair of polarities:

- Extroversion-Introversion: how an individual expresses energy

- Sensing-Intuition: how an individual perceives information

- Thinking-Feeling: how an individual processes information

The *extrovert* expresses energy to the external world, while the *introvert* discharges energy toward his or her internal world.

The *sensing* type believes and relies on information he or she receives from the external world, while the *intuitive* type believes and relies on information received from his or her own internal or imaginative world.

The *thinking* type makes decisions based on logic, while the *feeling* type makes decisions based on emotion.

Many professional graphologists use these same typologies to categorize the personalities of the subjects whose handwriting they are studying. Typology is a useful way to see an immediate "big picture" of the person whose handwriting you are reviewing. From there, you can hone in on the subtle traits that make this individual (and his or her writing) unique. You get a sense not only of a writer's character but of his or her limitations too.

PEN POINT   The Myers-Briggs Type Indicator

In the 1940s the psychologist Katherine Cook Briggs and her daughter, Isabel Briggs Myers, also a psychologist, developed a personality test based on Jung's typology that has become one of the foremost assessment tests administered by businesses. To Jung's three sets of personality types they added judging and perceiving, which relate to how a person implements knowledge and information in the external world. The *judging* personality favors orderliness, structure, and decisiveness based upon internal knowledge, while the *perceiving* personality tends to improvise or seek new information.

Through a series of targeted questions, the Myers-Briggs Type Indicator, or MBTI, categorizes respondents into one of sixteen combinations of personality types, such as ENFJ (Extrovert Intuitive Feeling Judging) or ISTP (Introvert Sensing Thinking Perceiving). This assessment helps businesses determine an employee's (or potential employee's) general style pertaining to business, decision making, communications, conflict management, relationships, and so on. It also helps the individual learn more about his or her style, in order to choose the optimum career path based on his or her particular personality type and strengths.

Applying Typology to Handwriting

Let's take a look at how the Jungian personality types can be discovered within a person's handwriting.

Extroversion Versus Introversion

Signifying Handwriting Traits: Direction of Movement and Spacing

If you quickly had to define the terms *extrovert* and *introvert,* you'd likely respond that an extrovert is outgoing, bubbly, and sociable, while an introvert is shy, withdrawn, and perhaps a bit of a loner. These traits often apply, respectively, but the true descriptions—as developed by Jung—of extroversion and introversion are quite different. An extrovert is actually a person who seeks energy from *outside the self.* This is someone who tends to think out loud or use others as sounding boards for ideas or decisions. By contrast, an introvert is actually a person who *goes within* to seek energy. This is someone who is introspective, who uses internal impressions and reality to create ideas or seek solutions. An introvert's peace is sought and found within rather than through external stimulation—or what might be perceived as bombardment—of other people, places, or things. We all possess qualities of both the extrovert and the introvert, but we each have a preference toward one.

In order to determine whether someone is an extrovert or an introvert, first examine the movement in the handwriting. How do you do that? Look at the direction. Do the words, letters, and strokes tend toward the right or the left?

As we learned in Chapter 2, movement toward the right, or *right trend*, signifies extroversion or outgoingness. It also signifies relationship to the future and others. Movement toward the left, or *left trend,* signifies introversion or keeping more to oneself. It also signifies a relationship to the past.

Some right trend, extroverted signs in handwriting are a right slant, movement toward the right side of page, *t*'s that are crossed to the right, *i*'s that are dotted to the right, and loops and ending strokes that pull to the right. The handwriting also tends to be average or larger in size.

A right trend movement indicates personality traits such as the ability to speculate; open-mindedness; an outgoing personality; ease with people; the ability to inspire, motivate, and engage others; and reaching out toward one's goals and objectives.

above address and put to the address he

Some left trend, introverted signs in handwriting are a left slant, movement toward the left side of the page, *t*'s that are crossed to the left, *i*'s that are dotted to the left, and loops and ending strokes that pull to the left. The handwriting also tends to be smaller or slender in size.

A left trend movement indicates a person who keeps to himself or herself and is introspective (and retrospective)—someone who is resistant to change but does not give up easily.

Next, look at the *spacing*. Are the letters and words large and spread out? Is there a tendency toward expansion in the writing both horizontally and vertically? If there is a signature, is it set to the right of the page? Does the pace of the writing impress you as fast, fluid, and connected with a garland style? This is also indicative of an extroverted personality.

I thoroughly enjoyed your presentation, and was naturally pleased to learn of your positive predictions.

In the handwriting of an introvert, the opposite will be true. The letters and words will appear small, compact, and even crowded. The writing will be more concentrated and compressed. The pace of the writing will impress you as slow and restrained, with the likelihood of an arcade form of connection.

Sorry for the delay in getting this hand written note to you. I am in harden as I write and plan to be in France in mid July when I will be visiting with one of the two parties I mean to discuss your services with.

Analysis of an Extrovert Typology

GENERAL "STORMIN'" NORMAN SCHWARZKOPF
Military Leader: Extrovert

General Norman Schwarzkopf aggressively imposes himself on the page in a powerful writing pattern, demonstrating tremendous confidence and an extrovert typology.

World Peace !

Schwarzkopf's writing utterly dominates the space. The height of his upper zone signals that he is interested in ideas. The unevenness of the letters indicates that he has many uncertainties and mood variations. He wants to rule. His illegible signature contains a strange, aggressive underline, upon which the letters rest. It looks like a Z, as in the mark of Zorro, with two powerful angles in it as well. This underline moves forcefully to the right. In this way Schwarzkopf creates his own world, reality, and fiefdom, which define him, forming a boundary as well as an emphasis on him.

He is a leader rather than a diplomat. Being more strategic than tactical, he has the courage of his convictions and will stand up for what he believes and pay the price if called upon. An example: Schwarzkopf risked his life to save soldiers in Vietnam. In Vietnam, the generals had their own parties, danced with pretty Red Cross nurses, and had luxuriously appointed apartments. Schwarzkopf, however, lived a Spartan existence, ate with his men, and socialized with them. Like General Patton, he was on the front lines. In other words, Schwarzkopf is committed to whatever he does and has immense vitality, power, and life force—he is a complex man of extremes for whom it is impossible to remain indifferent.

Analysis of an Introvert Typology

DR. JAMES WATSON
Nobel Prize–winning Scientist: Introvert

Why is James Watson's writing considered that of an introvert typology? Notice the wide spaces between words, wide spaces between lines, and narrow spaces between letters. The letters are upright rather than slanted. The writing is upright (toward the self) rather than toward the right (or left) of the page. This is a clear sign of the introvert.

The openness of the writing, the wide space picture, and the empty spaces on the page show the large impact of the writer's interior life, as well as the clarity of this awareness. Watson lives very much within himself. He does not enjoy socializing or engaging in other people's problems. He resides in his own world of the intellect. The small letter size indicates that he will not be emotionally available. It is his intellect that is available, and he cannot be expected to be sensitive to the needs of others.

Personality Trait Review

Extrovert	Introvert
Enjoys interacting with the external world	Derives peace and pleasure from internal self
Finds stimulation through new situations	Finds stimulation through solitude and nature
Prefers interaction with others	Enjoys a quieter external life
Accepts the external world as reality	Trusts what comes from exploring own heart and mind

Handwriting Trait Review

Extrovert	Introvert
Large letters and words	Small letters and words
Expansive writing overtaking space on page	Narrow spaces between letters
Small spaces between words	Wide spaces between words
Right slant and trend	Upright slant
Garland connection	Arcade connection
Large signature, placed toward right	Small signature, often set to the left
Movement is fast, easy, and fluid	Movement is slow
Dynamic and spontaneous writing	Inhibited and restrained writing
Wide left margin	Narrowing left margin
Heavy pressure	Light pressure

Sensing Versus Intuitive

Signifying Handwriting Trait: Pressure

What is the manner by which we "take in" information? Some of us innately prefer concrete and factual information that we obtain and experience directly. This tendency toward the realistic, pragmatic, and expedient indicates a *sensing* perception. Sensing personalities are drawn to facts. They have a need for clarity and place value on matters of practical relevance. They are also most comfortable with the known and familiar. They embrace tradition and social structures. Sensing people prefer specifics and plans. They are sticklers for detail and focus on the here and now. They also feel and utilize their senses to the fullest; they trust only what they can see, feel, smell, touch, taste, and measure. They are sensual and physical beings, who appreciate the body and enjoy physical skills like sports, dancing, or working with their hands.

The opposite is true of those who have an *intuitive* perception. Intuitives look toward the future—to ideas, goals, and possibilities. They are imaginative, innovative, unconventional, and forward thinking. They have far-reaching visions of and fascination with what "can be." They gravitate to all things spiritual and esoteric. Intuitives are often talkative, charismatic, and inspiring. They like to stand out in a crowd, and they are are fun loving and excitable. Intuitives are also intellectual, high-energy people who favor mental or imaginative energy over physical energy. They are usually restless and bored by routines and mundane tasks.

In order to determine whether someone is a sensing or intuitive personality, start by examining the pressure of ink on the page. The handwriting of a sensate is usually heavy and unvarying in pressure, compact, often stylized, and stable. There is also marked difference between the sizes of zones.

In all my years of scientific research, I have never seen a project that offers more hope for mankind than the one now underway in our laboratories.

The handwriting of an intuitive is light, rhythmic, and often uneven. It has a gentle pressure but tends toward irregularity: syllables or words can be disconnected, and if there are connections, they tend to be unusual in form. The upper zone is tall, and upper loops can bend back or to the left.

Analysis of a Sensing Typology
JACQUELINE KENNEDY ONASSIS
Former First Lady: Sensate

Jacqueline Kennedy Onassis was a sensate typology who used her five senses to the fullest. Her writing is deliberate and a little artificial in that she constructed it in a thoughtful, calculated manner. Her leftward slant shows independence and fortitude.

Sensates are often self-sufficient perfectionists who instinctively know what is right for the moment. Jackie insisted on order and protocol. She would be most fully alive when engaged in a totally involving sensual experience.

This is not an emotional writing. It is not rounded, but it has a lot of space between words; the letters going into the lower zone represent her enjoyment of material things as a substitute for feelings. She used highly simplified forms, which are precise and rigid. The emphasis on the lower zone—the zone of money and material possessions—reveals her aesthetic sensibility and sensuality as well.

This is a form-conscious writing, and to Jackie, seeing was believing. She liked things that were concrete, revealed in each carefully articulated letter. She enjoyed order and organization and wanted to be masterful in execution. She missed nothing in the details of the writing. She knew how to express and project who she was and how to get what she wanted when she wanted it.

The most legible letters are the initial ones. Most of her initial letters are separated deliberately in each stroke. This shows her lack of trust and an inability to connect emotionally to all but those closest to her.

Jackie was ambitious, as seen in her high upper zone. Sensates are pragmatic and expedient, and the clarity of her writing—the lack of embellishment and elaboration seen in her minimal letterforms—shows that she was efficient. She saw things clearly, and her focus helped her accomplish her goals. There is a clever use of space and many words in which the initial letter is strongly emphasized, a testament to the importance she placed on presentation.

She needed everything to look perfect and, unlike the intuitive, valued the social structure and order from which she came. Jackie's stroke is moderately pastose, which also means she had an appreciation of that which pleases the senses.

Analysis of an Intuitive Typology

NAPOLEON BONAPARTE
French Emperor: Intuitive

Intuitives are uninterested in social structures and like to stand apart from the crowd so they can create their own rules. Napoleon not only stood apart but above and beyond, and this was how he compensated for his damaged ego, which is seen in the small middle zone and the final, embellished stroke under his name. This paraph represents a need to remind the reader of his importance; it is, in effect, a pedestal on which he placed himself.

Intuitives are also highly excitable and easily distracted. They are always anticipating what is going to happen and are eager to go forward to implement their plans. The intuitive's awareness is best defined as knowing something without having to study it formally. Napoleon was blessed with awareness of what his adversaries were going to do and how to outmaneuver them—this is seen in the extreme speed and interesting connectors in the upper zone. The movement toward the right of the page also shows his drive.

Napoleon's use of space, his neglect and illegibility in the middle zone, as well as the speed and rhythm of the writing, show him able to perceive things that others could not see. He acted quickly on this intuition. This trait resulted in an enormous ability to conquer, manipulate, and achieve, which is visible in his signature.

Napoleon's hasty, illegible writing shows individuality and originality. It also reflects ambition and imagination, coupled with a lack of conscientiousness and duplicity. You can see these traits in the small script and the signature's unusual flourish, the energy and ambition of ascending lines and t-bars, the aspiring, tall upper loops, and the changeability of the letters.

Napoleon's original connections and strong forward movement reveal his tremendous vision and direction. He was extremely driven, seen in the energy and pressure of the stroke.

This is very high upper zone writing, emphasizing his creative fantasy. Although Napoleon was indifferent to practical aspects of tasks, he remained a great strategist and tactician. But he was more interested in the payoff of his objectives than in the process of reaching them.

Napoleon disregarded consequences and had swift and strong reactions to people and things, shown in the highly impulsive breaks in the writing, its speed, and the neglect of form. The writing reveals rapid shifts in mood. Different forms used for individual letters indicate inconstancy; this was a man loyal only to his own needs. Avarice is indicated in the way the letters crowd against one another. The pastose appearance expresses strong passions. Emotional extravagance is reflected by the different angles of the baseline; cruelty by the thick, clublike finals; focus and leadership traits by the small writing.

Personality Trait Review

Sensing	Intuitive
Present-oriented	Future-oriented
Uses five senses to the fullest	Highly imaginative and visionary
Sensual	Charismatic and charming
Most comfortable with the known and familiar	Attracted to spiritual matters
Favors "seeing is believing"	Likes to stand apart from the crowd
Enjoys physical skills and sports	Favors mental energy over physical
Pragmatic and efficient	Fun loving and excitable
Values social structures	Indifferent to social structures

Handwriting Trait Review

Sensing	Intuitive
Heavy, steady pressure	Light, gentle pressure
Medium to large writing	Airy and open writing
Emphasis in lower zone	Tall upper zone
Connected writing that's compact and dense	Simplified, varied connective form or disconnections
Slow movement	Moderate to quick movement
Right slant and trend	Uneven, irregular, illegible
Pastose strokes	Curved lower loops

Thinking Versus Feeling

Signifying Handwriting Traits: Size and Width

When we receive information, how do we process it? Carl Jung believed that people interpret either by a cause-and-effect, analytical, or *thinking* mode or by a more accommodating, value-based, or *feeling* mode. The thinking type places importance on personal experience of logic, while the feeling type emphasizes how personal likes or dislikes influence outcomes.

Those who are thinking types are often logical, analytical, and critical. They tend to question and probe. They have a natural propensity for seeking out and substantiating information they receive. They are intellectually driven, organized, and decisive, and place a lot of emphasis on timing and pacing. Structure and order are also very important to thinking types. They make plans and stick to them. In fact, they can get very distressed when things do not go according to their schedules.

The head rules the heart of thinking types. They often protect their emotions and vulnerabilities by channeling them to more intellectual pursuits. They can be very self-critical and uncomfortable dealing with the emotions of others.

The opposite is true of feeling types, who place more trust in their emotions than their thoughts. They are highly sensitive and prone to being hurt. Their perceptions reflect their personal values and tend to consider how outcomes affect other individuals. Feeling types place a high value on human relationships. They are considerate and responsive to the needs and feelings of others. They are loyal and devoted, have many friends, and thrive on emotional intimacy. Feeling types also place value on the past and are nostalgic. Memories of the past and childhood affect their present lives.

The handwriting of a thinking personality is usually small and simplified. It is organized, well spaced, and connected, the letters are rounded, and the style tends to be orderly and concentrated. It is also fast and light.

SEVERE EARTHQUAKE WEST USA, JAPAN
CLIMATIC #CHANGES MANY PARTS OF THE WORLD

CHINA BECOMES DOMINANT POWER IN ASIA
RELIGIOUS PROBLEMS ACUTE, MINOR
WARS.
WATER PROBLEMS ACCENTUATED AND
PARTIALLY SOLVED
DEMOCRACY UNDER SEVERE DILUTION
COMPUTER ERA, TOSS UP IF BENEFICIAL
SEVERE OVERPOPULATION PROBLEMS AND
UNEMPLOYMENT PROBLEMS WILL AFFECT
MANY COUNTRIES

The handwriting of a feeling personality is usually large and expansive, consistently slants to the right, and uses garlands as connectors. The style, in general, is soft and round.

The real heroes are men and women who are friends of the poorest of the poor.

* * *

DID YOU KNOW?

Many of America's "Founding Fathers" were thinking types. These include James Madison, Thomas Jefferson, John Adams, and Alexander Hamilton.

* * *

Analysis of a Thinking Typology

BARBARA WALTERS
Television Personality: Thinking

Barbara Walters is a thinking type who is careful, organized, and logical in the implementation of letters. Her writing is structured, as is her daily schedule. She considers thinking easier than feeling, seen in the compactness of the writing. This narrow writing also reveals her emotional inhibition and shyness. The right slant means that she compensates for her shyness by reaching out to achieve her objectives. She presents herself as more outgoing than she actually is, and in holding back her feelings, she can have control of what she shares with others.

Walters reveres the intellect. She uses her intelligence primarily and effectively but is not comfortable with her emotional side. The lower zone is highly attenuated. This is a very connected writing, which confirms her ability to deal with her emotions through logic.

Barbara Walters is analytical and pragmatic. There is a great deal of angularity here for a woman's writing. She is a perfectionist whose ambition is cloaked in the sensibility and appearance of softness, which may be why celebrities choose her over other interviewers. Behind this mask of sensitivity, however, is firm control. There is a lot of compulsiveness in the writing and the letters are more contracted than released. Although she is known for being sensitive to others' feelings when she conducts an interview, she is clearly not in touch with her own emotions. This is seen by the space picture and the narrowness of the letterforms.

Personal discipline is her watchword, and the writing can also be interpreted as hoarding—she doesn't care as much about love as she does about acquisition.

Analysis of a Feeling Typology

ELIZABETH TAYLOR
Actress: Feeling

How does Elizabeth Taylor's writing reveal that she is a feeling type? The initial letters are overdone, filled with circularity and emotion, and they seem to rush forward. She loves always to be experiencing and indulging her emotional weather vane. Although her writing is very connected, she doesn't always want or like to think things through.

Taylor reaches her goals through willpower rather than vitality, as seen again in the overconnection of the letters. Everything points to her need for self-expression. She knows how to communicate who she is very clearly. The letters most legible are the initial ones, confirming her love of presentation. The contraction shows enormous tension, the size and embellishment of her initial letters confirm her narcissism.

She is indulgent, moody, and volatile, confirmed by the uneven baseline of her writing. She finds it difficult to interrupt an emotion once she gets involved with it—or with someone—and we see this once again in the connectedness of her writing.

Taylor overwhelms others and, in turn, is overwhelmed by them. Everything for her is overdone and demonstrative. The lack of restraint in her writing shows that her intellect is guided by emotions as it moves powerfully to the right of the page.

Personality Trait Review

Thinking	Feeling
Craves structure, order	Feels emotions rule
Needs to understand "why" things happen	Nostalgic about the past
Ruled by the head	Ruled by the heart
Deep love of justice	Great sensitivity to others
Decisive	Hurt easily, prone to self-pity
Great organizational skills	Values human relationships, intimacy
Intellectual and scholarly	Needs to belong
Verbal and writing strength	Devoted and loyal

Handwriting Trait Review

Thinking	Feeling
Small, rounded letters	Large writing
Spare and simple	Broad letters
Creative connections	Garland or angular writing
Light pressure	Medium pressure
Short lower zone	Large middle zone

Guess Who?

A Typology Quiz

Now let's practice what you've learned. Each of the following samples reflects one of the six personality types. Review each sample on the left and match it with its typology on the right. Take your time and have fun! Feel free to review the chapter for more information.

Sample	**Type**
1. *[handwritten sample]*	A. Extrovert
2. *[handwritten sample]*	B. Introvert
3. *[handwritten sample]*	C. Sensing
4. *[handwritten sample]*	D. Intuitive
5. *[handwritten sample]*	E. Thinking

---

* The circle in the third line of the sample was placed for emphasis. It was not in the original handwriting

6.

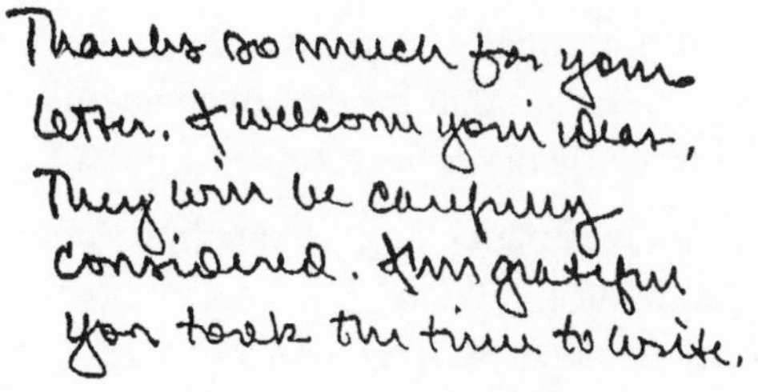

[handwritten text]

F. Feeling

Answers

1. *F—Feeling* This handwriting belongs to **Mary Stuart, Queen of Scots.**

   Mary was skillful with a quill, the preferred writing instrument of her time, and well trained in penmanship. You can see a lot of emotional variation in the size of her letters and in the variable baseline. These changes show great sensitivity and mood swings. Her writing reveals a warm and devoted person who was careful about accurately communicating her rich thoughts and feelings to others. Like most feeling types, Mary was ruled by her heart rather than her head. She valued human relationships and intimacy above all else.

   The size and regularity of Mary's writing is consistent, which demonstrates that she was loyal and devoted and had a need to belong—all characteristics of the feeling type. The drifting t-bars indicate a character easily influenced by others and swept away by emotions. The writing slants down at the right margin, again indicating her emotional currents and changes of mood. The large letters and broad strokes are also testaments to the feeling type.

2. *D—Intuitive* This handwriting belongs to the composer **Ludwig van Beethoven.**

   Intuitives are forward thinking. We can see that Beethoven looked toward the future because his writing moves toward the right. He was imaginative, as seen in the height and loops in his upper zone, and innovative, as seen in the creative chaos of his handwriting form—he broke the rules for the written etiquette of his era by creating his own forms. If you look closely, you can see that his writing almost resembles musical notation. His connective forms are also unusual, testament to his brilliance. It is even more impressive to realize that Beethoven could only hear this music in his head (because of his deafness).

3. *E—Thinking*   This handwriting belongs to the third American president, **Thomas Jefferson.**

The simplicity of Jefferson's writing speaks to his having been a thinking man. In an era when most writing possessed florid embellishments, Jefferson's simple and well-proportioned letters show his originality and intellect. In fact, the spacing, structure, and form level in his writing all confirm that he was ahead of his time. His finely developed sense of space on the page is indicative of his ability to negotiate his world.

Jefferson was logical and critical, as revealed in the dryness and sparseness of his letters. The writing is very well organized, and there is a lot of clarity and balance—an obvious reflection of how his mind worked. He was organized and disciplined, detail-oriented, someone who got all the facts and sides of an issue before making a decision.

Jefferson's small middle zone and contracted writing shows his discomfort in dealing with the emotions of others—he was a true thinker rather than feeling type.

4. *C—Sensing*   This handwriting belongs to the American statesman, inventor, and diplomat **Benjamin Franklin.**

Franklin had very connected writing, showing him to be a logical, sensing type. The pastose (heavy) strokes and steady pressure reveal that he had sensory awareness and delighted in the sensual world. The writing is small but with large initial letters, which shows he was proud of himself and his accomplishments. The extreme right slant and lyrical *d* confirm his skills as a diplomat and writer.

The use of space is extraordinarily well organized. This is a reflection of Franklin's clarity of thinking and understanding of what was happening around him. The regularity in the writing shows he had high standards and integrity. The writing is small and analytical, revealing an unusual security in his ability to understand things.

5. *B—Introvert*   This handwriting belongs to the comedian **Joe Piscopo.**

This former *Saturday Night Live* star's small letters and compact words, along with his upward slant, show him to be inhibited and restrained in his private life. The movement of the writing is slow, with moderate to wide spaces between words, which means he keeps others at bay. Wide margins indicate self-protection—these are common qualities of the introverted type.

Like many comedians, Piscopo is a born introvert who likely grew to display more qualities of an extrovert to gain a competitive edge in his field.

6. *A—Extrovert*   This handwriting belongs to the former president **Bill Clinton.**

It's no surprise that Clinton is an extrovert. His large letters and words make his handwriting expansive. The writing is dynamic and spontaneous, fast and fluid, with pastose strokes indicating his sexual appeal and sensuality. This is a man who definitely thrives on interactions with others and the external world. He finds new situations and experiences stimulating, challenging, and necessary.

Even though Clinton is left-handed and his letters are more upward, you can almost feel the rightward movement.

Score

1–2   Take more time. You'll get there.

3–4   Off to a good start.

5–6   You're an excellent graphologist-in-training.

Practice Tips

Don't be discouraged if you did not score 5 or 6. Practice by collecting samples from people you know. See if you can identify their true types!

CHAPTER 4

The Write Stuff

*   *   *

HOW TO GET AND READ
HANDWRITING SAMPLES

*Now it's time to take what you've learned and apply it!
This chapter provides tips on how to collect writing
samples and begin analyzing handwriting.
Actual samples will be used to illustrate styles
and techniques. Collecting autographs and
interpreting signatures will be covered in this chapter
as well. Charts and checklists will also be included
to help you record your findings and begin
analyzing your samples.*

"Excuse me—how do I get to Carnegie Hall?"
"Practice!"

—HENNY YOUNGMAN

BY NOW, you're probably thinking to yourself, I had no idea that
a handwriting sample could hold so many clues to the writer's personality. So, obviously, you're eager to take this newfound
knowledge and apply it. How do you start?

Practice makes perfect. The more samples you collect and the
more time you spend reviewing them, the more patterns you will
begin to discern. When developing this new skill, you will likely
have to keep referring back to this book, or your own notes, to refresh your mind with all the various handwriting characteristics
and what they mean. It might feel a bit overwhelming at first—
there are so many details to consider! But, as in learning a new

language, in time the elements fall smoothly into place, and soon, with practice, your first impressions of a handwriting sample will become instinctive and your interpretations will increase in accuracy. It's simply a matter of time, effort, and practice.

To help the process along, charts and checklists are provided in this and other chapters. Do use them—they will prove handy and work to reinforce your knowledge.

Collecting Handwriting Samples

To begin analyzing handwriting, you'll need to obtain writing samples. So, if you haven't already done so, start collecting now. This won't be difficult and should be fun. In fact, it's likely that people will deluge you with samples once they know you're looking for them.

A good place to find handwriting samples is at home. Have you received any letters lately? Any birthday or holiday cards with handwritten notes? If you were away at college or in the military, or are a frequent traveler, are there any letters that you've saved from loved ones and friends? How about a love letter or two that you kept for nostalgic reasons? Check your desk, home files, or the attic.

PEN POINT Keeping It Confidential

Some of you may wonder if it's right or ethical to analyze a handwriting sample without the writer's permission. If you were to become a professional graphologist, you would follow a definitive Code of Ethics (see "Code of Ethics for Graphologists").

However, chances are you are interested in graphology as a hobby. As long as you're doing this for your personal enjoyment and not profiting from your analysis, not using the information you derive in a negative or hurtful way, and not making your assessments or judgments public in any manner that can be deemed slanderous, as a beginner you can feel at ease examining the handwriting of others.

In general, it's best to keep your analyses confidential or directed solely to the person whose handwriting you are reviewing and remember to stress that at this time you are a student of graphology.

If you don't have any writing samples on hand, ask for some. Don't be shy! Call upon friends and family members, colleagues at work, your baby-sitter or housekeeper, your roommate, your doctor, dentist, professor, building superintendent, hairdresser, or even your personal trainer—anyone with whom you come in contact and feel comfortable asking. Before you know it, those samples will start piling up! And when they do, create a file or get a box in which to store them safely—you don't want to leave them in a place where they can get lost or damaged.

PEN POINT   It's Not Child's Play

Until the age of twenty-one, human beings are technically still developing and maturing. The same goes for their handwriting! Therefore, children and most teens will display traits in their writing that, while acceptable in youngsters, would be considered "red flags" in the writing of adults. So, in order to avoid mistaken conclusions, it is best for you now to focus on analyzing handwriting samples of adults.

How to Ask for a Handwriting Sample

Here's an approach to asking for a handwriting sample that I've used successfully—especially when the person whose writing I desired was someone of merit or distinction. At an appropriate moment, start up a conversation about any topic you think might be engaging. During this pleasant exchange, politely say, "Would you consider providing me with a sample of your writing? I'm studying creativity in writing and collecting writings of interesting personalities. I would be delighted to learn more about you by examining your handwriting." You must stress that this is a relatively new subject for you, and the results will be kept confidential (and you must keep your word!).

When presented this way, your request will likely intrigue and please the person you're asking, making it more likely that he or she will comply.

"What Should I Write?"

People will almost always be amenable to giving you samples of their writing, but they frequently get stumped about *what* to write. Here are some ideas you might suggest:

- Write about something that happened to you today or yesterday.
- Write about someone you care about.
- Write a quick letter or note to someone.
- Write about something you're looking forward to doing.
- Write about an issue you feel passionate about.
- Write about a favorite memory or experience.
- Write about your ideas or goals for the coming year.
- Write about an unforgettable experience you wish to relive.

The most common types of material you're likely to get when someone spontaneously meets your request for a writing sample are notes that say, "Here is a sample of my handwriting. I can't wait to see what this reveals about me" and "The quick brown fox jumped over the lazy dog" or "Now is the time for all good men to come to the aid of their country," or some other common statement that the writer can jot down without much thought. Whatever gets written, it's best to have a page's worth of writing—the more material you have, the more insight you'll get.

Format and Medium

When attempting a handwriting analysis, it is important to obtain an original sample of writing, rather than a photocopy or a fax (these technologies can often distort letter formations), or you'll miss the pressure, vitality, and energy.

Ideally, one should have a sample written with a ballpoint or fountain pen on an 8½-by-11-inch sheet of unlined paper. Unlined is preferable because the lines on ruled paper can influence direction of the writing, and other types of pens do not discharge ink in the same way that a regular ballpoint or fountain pen would. People who do not like any friction between the pen point and the page often use felt-tipped pens, but these instruments do not permit the pressure of the writing to be properly evaluated.

And, whenever possible, have the writer sign the sample at the end. Signatures are our psychological calling cards, the way in which we wish to be seen by others. If you are very lucky, you might ask for more than one sample, to see how the writing has changed over time.

An Important Note About Signatures

Although signatures may often be the easiest samples to obtain, they are limited in scope. Whenever you can, get a whole page of writing—at least ten sentences—as well as the signature.

What Handwriting Can—and Cannot—Reveal

When you collect a handwriting sample, it is important to know the writer's nationality and handedness, as well as gender and age. "But I thought that a good graphologist can find out everything about a person by looking at the handwriting?" you ask.

The basic qualities a professional graphologist can see in handwriting are personality type and traits, energy level, and potential at the time that sample was penned. What cannot be discerned are traits like gender or sexual orientation, age, ethnicity, nationality (unless, of course, the sample submitted is written in the individual's native language), religion, political affiliation, insidious health issues, or what will happen to the writer in the future. This is why graphology is a popular tool in hiring—it is nondiscriminating.

While handwriting might reveal a person's potential, it cannot reveal likes, dislikes, or interests. There might be artistic or mathematical ability shown in the handwriting, but what cannot be seen is whether the writer is artistic in music, art, writing, or dance, or whether he's a scientist, accountant, or mathematician. Neither does this inherent ability seen in writing guarantee the writer's vocation.

PEN POINT   Handwriting Stereotypes

Don't be fooled. Beautifully embellished and legible handwriting is not indicative of gender. You'd be surprised by how many men have handwriting that may appear feminine or women whose writing shows masculine tendencies. These qualities do not in any way denote strength, weakness, or sexual orientation.

Illegible handwriting is not indicative of a troubled personality (think of how illegibly most doctors write!) nor is "perfect penmanship" indicative of a stable, graceful, or upstanding individual.

The more you learn about graphology, the more you'll come to see that general (and untrained) perceptions of handwriting are incorrect. You can now take pride and comfort in knowing that the next time you're with people who make naïve assumptions about others on the basis of their handwriting, you'll be able to set them right.

May I Have Your Autograph?

While compiling a collection of writing samples, you might find yourself coming into the possession of autographs from celebrities, politicians, athletes, and other notables, which might foster an interest in autograph and handwriting collecting. Many have made a fascinating and profitable hobby of this activity, so in case the collector's bug bites you, here are some tips for obtaining autographs and other handwriting samples from the famous or infamous.

- Network. Ask all the people you know if they have any famous autographs they can share with you or if they know or have access to any celebrity or notable who might be willing to provide an autograph.

- If you ever have an opportunity to hang out at the stage door of a Broadway theater or rock concert, or outside a sporting event locker room, you'll have a great chance to meet a celebrity and ask for an autograph.

- Politicians are easily accessible (especially while on the campaign trail) and are usually friendly and cooperative to supporters or constituents. Keep in mind that what you might learn about a candidate through his or her handwriting could affect your vote!

- Write letters to people you admire. Sometimes a simple, polite letter asking for an autograph or signed photograph gets results. If the person has written a book or has a CD, send this item along to be signed.

  Note: Be sure to include a self-addressed, stamped envelope (SASE) along with your request—the easier you make it for the person you're asking, the likelier he or she will be to oblige!

- Talk to booksellers. Many bookstores have regular book signings, which are great ways to get autographs. Many larger booksellers stock signed editions of books that you can purchase. Buying such books is a great way to collect a signature from a notable author.

- Do a search on eBay. This Internet auction site is a clearinghouse for all sorts of great stuff, autographs included.

- Memorabilia shows pop up in cities on a regular basis. For a modest entrance fee, you can rub elbows with athletes and film and TV stars, and purchase autographed photos, books, posters, and other items. As the contact is more personal, you might be able to turn on the charm and get the celebrity to write an extra line or two.

- Reputable auction houses frequently purchase historical letters, documents, and signatures that they sell to serious collectors. Here's where you are apt to find the signatures of people like Napoleon, Benjamin Franklin, Franklin Roosevelt, and other famous figures whose writing is rare and valuable. Be prepared to spend some money at these venues.

Last, hang on to what you collect. Maybe that teenager next door who's captain of the high school football team will turn out to be an NFL pro; or that aspiring actress in your community theater will become a cast member of a hot TV show—you never know what these documents might be worth down the line.

Interpreting the Signature

Your signature is your psychological calling card, the image you wish to convey to others, your public persona. It also represents the way you would like others to respond to you.

Whenever you sign your name, you leave behind a symbolic reflection of who you are. Once we've developed our signatures, they generally remain consistent throughout our lives, unless we undergo major life changes. Signatures can also be altered by age, illness, stress, medication, and mood swings.

If signatures represent our public images, our other writing (general text) provides a glimpse into our personal images. That's why it is always preferable to obtain a writing sample that contains both text and signature. Not everyone acts the same in public as in private. When you create long-form samples of writing, you are basically communicating ideas and feelings. But when it comes to your signature, you're communicating your public image. Text that is comparable with the signature shows that our public personae are in tune with our private perceptions of ourselves; text that is in contrast to the signature suggests duality—that we might have something to hide or we are hiding from something.

Looking for "Signs" in Signatures

If you're fortunate enough to obtain a sample that contains both text *and* a signature, you can apply some of the following guidelines to gain insight into the personality of the individual whose handwriting you are reviewing.

- **Consistency Between the Signature and the Writing**
  If the signature is consistent with the rest of the writing (meaning that the style variables in the signature resemble those in the text), what you see is what you get. This is an individual whose public and private personalities are one and the same. This is a person who has little to hide, who is consistent and likely dependable.

- **Signature Slightly Larger Than Rest of Writing**
  This writer has a healthy self-presentation.

- **Signature Much Larger Than Rest of Writing**
  This writer needs to be seen and heard. He is usually insecure but overcompensates by coming on strong to gain attention and build his ego; or she could be a public figure who has practiced a signature that she believes best reflects her public persona or the expectations of others.

- **Signature Slightly Smaller Than Rest of Writing**
  This writer is shy, reserved, insecure, and not comfortable in large groups. He'd prefer to remain in the background rather than attract attention.

- **Signature Much Smaller Than Rest of Writing**
  This writer is someone who wants attention but attracts it—by making herself small and unnoticeable so that others seek her out.

- **Upright Signature with Right-Slanting Writing**
  This writer is cool and aloof in public but warmer and more approachable in private.

- **Right-Slanting Signature with Upright Writing**
  This writer is warm and friendly to others in public but cool and aloof in private.

- **Legible Signature with Legible Writing**
  When all aspects of writing are clear and legible, the writer can be who he is to others and communicate well.

- **Legible Writing with Illegible Signature**
  This is a person who is willing to convey her thoughts clearly but doesn't want to convey much about who she really is.

If all you are able to obtain is a signature, the following guidelines will help you interpret that autograph.

- **Legible Signature**
  The person feels good about himself and has nothing to hide.

- **Illegible Signature**
  An illegible signature is frequently the result of the writer being busy or in a rush. There are also people (celebrities, athletes, doctors, lawyers, corporate bigwigs, and so on) who have to sign their names so many times in a day that they simply scribble thier signatures out hastily and illegibly. However, if a signature is illegible for a reason other than haste, chances are this is an individual who would prefer to conceal her true nature.

- **Inclusion of Middle Name or Middle Initial**
  If a signature contains the person's middle name or initial, it usually indicates that the writer is proud or more formal about his public presentation.

- **Last Name Larger Than First Name**
  A last name larger than the first name shows pride in the writer's family name (or, for a woman who is married and takes her husband's last name, regard for her husband's family).

- **First Name Larger Than Last Name**
  A first name larger than the last name reveals someone who is proud of his or her accomplishments, but may have issues with a parent or key family member. If a married woman has issues with her husband, she might right her last name much

smaller than her first name or write her last name on a separate line.

- **Illegible Last Name**
  An illegible last name indicates that the writer may have issues with his or her parents.

- **Illegible First Name**
  An illegible first name indicates that a writer may have an insecure ego.

Fancy Signatures

Curls, swirls, underlines, and other decorative touches that embellish a signature have their own meaning. The simpler and less adorned the signature, the more secure the individual.

* * *

DID YOU KNOW?

Any embellishment placed beneath a signature is called a *paraph*.

* * *

- **Embellished Signature**
  An embellished signature shows a person who needs recognition or attention.

- **Underlined Signature**
  An underlined signature reveals a person who is proud, emphasizing self-image.

- **Circle Around Signature or Covered Signature**
  A signature with a circle around it or one that is covered shows that the writer is either hiding something or has a need to protect himself or herself.

- **Crossed Signature**
  If the last stroke in a signature is crossed back over the name, the person has conflicts and may wish to separate from others, including family.

A Look at Famous Signatures

One fascinating place to begin looking at the hidden personalities behind signatures is signatures of famous people. Examine the following signatures and see what conclusions you come to about the men or women behind them. Then read the analyses and see how accurate you are!

JOAN COLLINS (Actress)

Everything in Joan Collins's writing is overdone and very dramatic; it has an attention-getting quality. The excess circularity in the writing shows that she overemotes and is filled with fantasy and energy. We can see that she is very self-involved because she leaves no space between the letters and inflates the capitals. One would not suspect that she was originally an introvert, for now she knows the world outside her better than her inner world. Collins was destined to be a diva, and her writing is filled with stardust!

CINDY CRAWFORD (Model)

Cindy Crawford is a clever woman who writes with fluency, liquidity, and a notable right trend. Her writing reveals her competence through the speed, rhythm, ease, and movement to the right. These qualities show she has the necessary energy and enthusiasm to pursue her objectives. There is a beautiful connection between the *w* and the *f* in *Crawford*, a sign of efficiency and intellect. This gesture, which is highly aesthetic and stylish, shows her affinity for form and beauty. Crawford could have been a designer in any of the decorative arts.

John Grisham (Author)

John Grisham's writing reveals a lot of fantasy and an ability to explore his inner life, as manifested by the huge lower loops. His unconscious is replete with images, but Grisham's writing creates images that do not remain unconscious for long. He also has very spiky, almost combative writing. It is illegible but creates a dynamic appearance. There is also some articulate lettering filled with creativity. Part of his writing is organized, detailed, structured, compulsive, and analytic, while another part is filled with fantasy. He knows how to combine both elements.

Michael Jackson (Pop Music Icon)

Michael Jackson's signature is designed like a logo. Notice how he balances the last stroke of the *M* in *Michael* with the last stroke of the *J* in *Jackson*—he wants to maintain the same proportion. The design at the end of the name looks a bit like a spider, but there is a stylish quality to the signature overall.

The last stroke of the *M* in *Michael* shoots way up. That reveals Jackson's sense of self-importance. The huge *l* in *Michael*, which encircles the *J* in *Jackson*, confirms this. However, the *n* in *Jackson* reaches up and then drops down with force into the lower zone—the line seems to block off his connection to other people like a wall, keeping him from dealing with the outside world.

The loop that encircles the *J* in *Jackson* is like a cocoon, protecting it. Jackson wants his public image to be one thing, while his personal image remains private and protected.

STEPHEN KING (Author)

King is a highly introverted person who spends much time accessing his "inner theater." His writing pattern is compressed, perhaps representing or resulting in his dark stories. Look at the *g* in *King*, where the lower zone distortion hints at disturbed fantasies coming from the unconscious, which may reflect traumatic events in his early life. There is a tremendous amount of internal pressure and intensity in this signature. King's writing represents someone who is very logical, as seen in the extremely connected letters and strong emphasis on the upper zone. It seems difficult for him to find release through this zone, which represents his creative fantasies. The big loop that comes from the end of the *Stephen* and circles around his first name is also the realm of his fantasy, his private space, where he works out his original thought streams. This is a perfect illustration of the symbolism of his private fantasies.

BILL MARRIOTT (Hotel Entrepreneur)

Bill Marriott is a businessman, with the writing of an extrovert. The signature is very sophisticated, rapid, yet delicately executed. There are breaks after the *B* in *Bill* and the *M* in *Marriott,* signifying a pause to check out data before making a final decision. Once Marriott makes the decision to move, however, he does so with implacable force.

The pressure of the writing is strong, which indicates great vitality. In the two *t*'s in *Marriott,* the bar is slightly above the stems of both *t*'s, which means his reach can exceed his grasp. He has very big visionary plans. The second t-stem in *Marriott* (like the second *l* in *Bill*) is larger than the first, which means he moves himself forward with energy and determination.

As we know, the upper zone represents our creative fantasy and aspiration, and the lower zone represents money and instincts. Marriott emphasizes the upper and lower zones in his writing. The *M* in *Marriott* goes down into the lower zone, but there is a strong aesthetic quality to it, an ability to flow with whatever the energetic current is at the moment, confirmed by an adaptable, adjustable, fluid movement throughout the writing.

JOE PESCI (Actor)

Joe Pesci's signature is the writing of a very intense man, seen in the overblown *J* which encircles the *o,* covering it and making it look like a knot. The *J* is an enlargement of himself on the page. This signature is driven and focused. There is strong pressure. The

P is written very quickly, meaning he is too impatient to complete his name—he just implements the *P*. Likewise, the i-dot is marked, but not over the *i*. In his last name and in the phrase *God is Good*, Pesci's i-dots are free-flowing fantasies, floating through the air—a sign of creativity. Overall, however, the writing is well organized, smooth, and elegant, not always congruent with many of the roles Pesci plays.

RIVER PHOENIX (Actor)

The signature of River Phoenix looks like a Chinese ideogram and is clearly unconventional. Phoenix wants to project an elaborate identity, and the time and thought he put into his signature is quite impressive. His persona is complex and not easy to penetrate. It is also somewhat mysterious and aesthetic; it is almost as if he has designed a logo for his identity rather than actually having an identity. He wants to appear more challenging and mysterious than he may be. His signature is a façade that he presents so others will never know him or see his vulnerability. His interior conflict is seen in the garland and circular forms.

ROBERT REDFORD (Actor and Director)

Robert Redford has a conservative writing style. He closes his letters off at the end of the signature, which appears as a shieldlike form of self-protection. This is a very sensitive writing with elegant and fluid forms. The endings of his words create attention and give the writing significance.

Redford presents a strong, rhythmic writing, very fast and smooth.The longer you look at it, the clearer it appears. The line underneath his name forms the baseline, so there is a clear ground for him to stand on, as if it is a delineation of a secure boundary. But, the writing is also a graceful and charming expression with strong movement to the right, toward goals still to be realized. The speed and confidence in the writing confirm that he knows where he is going and how to get there. Both the *r* and the *d* in *Redford* are unusual. And he integrates the *Robert* with the *Redford* as if they are one word. The formation of *Red* in *Redford* is an expression of his individuality. This is the creative, original letter pattern of a man who has it all together.

MARTIN SCORSESE (Director)

Martin Scorsese is a driven man who knows how to reach his goals. His signature is beautiful, intense, fluid, and direct. He is confident, efficient, and anxious to get on with his agenda. The writing is effective. It has speed and rhythm, but there is also a diminuendo by the end of the letters that shows sensitivity toward others. Scorsese's signature is evolved, complex, and thoughtful.

SISSY SPACEK (Actress)

For a female small in stature, Sissy Spacek has a huge and powerful signature. It appears almost masculine, with great energy to move to wherever she wants to go. She is not one to be easily stopped. The signature is very angular, showing she knows how to make use of her creative force. Spacek has tremendous willpower and effectiveness. The *k* in *Spacek* is assertive, ending her name imposingly, which means "You are not going to push me around." Spacek stands up for herself at all costs. She is conscientious and can become obsessive when driving toward her goals and needs. This is seen in the angularity and connection of the writing.

KEVIN SPACEY (Actor)

Through the huge capital letters, this cool and distant writing reveals narcissism but also self-awareness and sophistication. By the connections and the space picture, we see that Spacey is very aware of the world around him. He knows a lot and translates it into what serves him. The threadiness represents his efficiency and maneuverability. His creativity is seen by the second part of the *K,* which flows right into what purports to be the *Kevin.* Aesthetic, delicate, sensitive, and with very light pressure, this signature has elegance and grace, which give Spacey skill in adapting to challenges. We can see from his signature that he is a fine actor with a first-rate intellect.

STEVEN SPIELBERG (Director)

Steven Spielberg's writing becomes larger, which is a means of imposing himself on the page. The big *S* in *Steven* and in *Spielberg* means that he is filled with many large projects and plans.

In the words "Best Wishes," we see his detachment. The letters are disconnected yet brilliant. The writing is highly simplified, a testament to his intellect. The *t* in "Best Wishes" is large. The *h* is high into the upper zone, which is emphasized throughout his name, especially in his second signature.

In this second, less legible signature, in what purports to be a *g* we see a form almost like a scythe (a harvesting instrument)—possibly to cut out the opposition! The emphasis in the upper zone signifies ambition and a drive toward the future, fantasies, and creative aspiration. Spielberg lives in the world of the mind and is very happy there. He is filled with plans, activities, and ideas, resulting in little attention to the middle zone. We can see he is much more interested in the upper zone. Even the lower zone is attenuated. The writing is also entrepreneurial and filled with ideas and originality.

BARBRA STREISAND (Actress, Singer, and Director)

Barbra Streisand presents another huge signature. Look at the *B* in *Barbra*—it is very rhythmic and sophisticated. Even though the letters in *Streisand* are illegible, there is still a graceful flow, but the loop of the *d* drops into the lower zone, which bespeaks an inordinate interest in the material.

This is a very bright, spontaneous, aesthetically designed writing, except for the very large initial letters that are huge in proportion to the middle zone. Streisand knows who she is and expects you to know it as well. The t-bar in her last name is very powerful. It is her lance, so to speak, representing an aggressive, forceful application of her intellect. She pursues her objectives without compromise. The *d* ends with a distinct, imposing sense of a shield and resistance: "You are not going to put anything over on me!" At the top of the *Barbra* her signature curves back to itself, showing that she knows what she wants and returns, in the final analysis, to her own counsel.

ROBIN WILLIAMS (Comedian and Actor)

Robin Williams's mind works so fast that he doesn't have time to make his signature legible. He jots down what look like a distorted *R* and *W*. This signature is more a logo, a fleeting, ephemeral impression from one moment to another, with incredibly rapid sparks of movement, as if it is a performance.

This writing shows that Williams has no patience. The writing is also incredibly elegant and brilliantly rhythmic, even in its reduction of form. You cannot immediately identify the writer, but the letters reflect high intelligence and the ability to move and think like quicksilver on the page.

The Big Picture

You've now got your handwriting samples on hand and this book to guide you, so you're ready to tackle your first analysis. First, look at the sample carefully to gain a first overall impression. Keep these questions in mind:

- Does the writing seem weak or vital?
- Are the letters full or meager?
- Is the writing legible?
- How is the writing placed on the page?
- Is the writing thready, spiky, or rounded?

- Does the writing fill the page well, or are the margins wide?
- Does the movement of the writing seem fast or slow?

These questions—as well as other variables—help you to form an initial impression. Look at the writing with as much objectivity as possible. Illegible handwriting doesn't mean that the writer is someone you might find objectionable. In fact, someone whose handwriting looks sloppy or illegible might turn out to be a bright, creative person who's really worth knowing. Beethoven's handwriting in Chapter 3 seems quite chaotic—an untrained eye might think that sample was indicative of a troubled individual rather than a genius! More often than not, people with "perfect" school type handwriting are more defensive and hidden than their counterparts with bad penmanship!

Handwriting is like a landscape. The average person looking at a garden or field sees green, but a gardener sees tremendous variation and subtlety among the textures and shades. As you become more adept at knowing what to look at in a handwriting sample, you will see a written page in the same way the gardener sees the landscape.

PEN POINT   Form Level

When you begin an analysis, one of the things you immediately take into account is the writing's *form level*. This is a blanket term that graphologists use to encompass style, symmetry, simplicity, legibility, creativity, movement, and rhythm.

Reading Between the Lines

A typical line of writing can be quickly evaluated by using this simple template. It represents the "imaginary" lines, spaces, directions, and zones that you consider when "reading" a handwriting on a set line. This template was adapted from the book *ABC of Graphology* by Michel Moracchini, Editions Jacques Grancher, 1983.

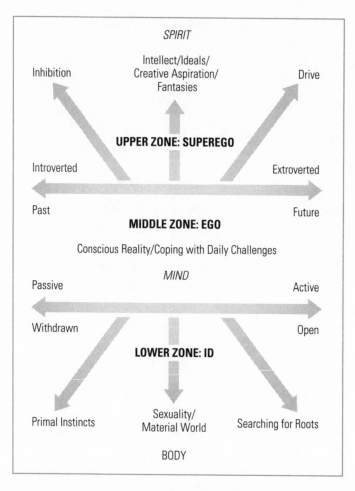

If you review the handwriting against this template, you'll get a good, general glimpse into the writer's key personality tendencies.

Graphology Worksheet

A good way to begin mastering the art of graphology is to use this worksheet as you study a handwriting sample. Make copies of the worksheet at the back of the book for future analyses and keep it handy. As you review a handwriting sample, you can record the various qualities and what they mean. At the end of the evaluation, you can look back at this worksheet to help you come to more educated conclusions.

Graphological Worksheet

Date: Name:

Gender: Male   Female

Circle the traits you see present in the sample you are evaluating.

Handwriting Qualities	Trait Specifics			Meaning
Margins				
Overall:	Balanced	Narrow	Wide	
Left Margin:	Consistently Narrow Consistently Wide Straight	Narrowing Widening Irregular		
Right Margin:	Consistently Narrow Consistently Wide Straight	Narrowing Widening Irregular		
Upper Margin:	Narrow	Wide		
Lower Margin:	Narrow	Wide		
Spacing				
Line Spacing:	Balanced Overlapping	Narrow Wide	Irregular	
Word Spacing:	Balanced Wide	Narrow Very Wide	Very Narrow Irregular	
Letter Spacing:	Balanced Narrow Wide Irregular Space after first letter			
Baseline	Steady	Wavy		
Zones	Upper Balanced	Middle	Lower	
Size	Small Varying	Medium	Large	
Connective Form	Garland Thread	Arcade	Angle	
Strokes	Downstroke School Type	Upstroke Sharp Stroke	Pastose	

Handwriting Qualities	Trait Specifics	Meaning
Connectiveness	Moderately Connected Highly Connected Overconnected Disconnected Printed	
Slant	Right Left Upright Variable	
Directional Movement	Right Trend Left Trend	
Rhythm	Strong Weak	
Form	Regular Legible Irregular/Illegible	
Speed	Slow Well Paced Fast Very Fast	
Pressure	Normal Heavy Light	
Signature		
Form:	Legible Illegible	
Size:	Small Medium Large	
Emphasis:	First name larger than last name Last name larger than first name First and last names of equal size	
Embellishment:	Crossed Circled Underlined Other None	
Balance:	Larger than text Smaller than text Balanced	
Typology	Extrovert Introvert Sensing Intuitive Thinking Feeling	

Overall Impression:

Conclusion:

Putting It All Together

Let's review the process of creating a personality picture for anyone whose handwriting you are reviewing.

1. Obtain a writing sample, preferably written with a ballpoint or fountain pen on unlined paper. If the sample you obtain has both paragraphs and a signature, so much the better.

2. Examine the sample closely and use the Graphological Worksheet to help you make notes about its unique characteristics.

3. After selecting the traits on the worksheet, if you need to, refer back through the book or your own notes to record the meaning of each trait.

4. When you have recorded the meaning of each trait, make notes about your overall impression of the sample, including of the subject's personality "type."

5. Finally, note your conclusions in the space provided.

The Graphological Key at the back of this book provides another resource for studying or looking up handwriting traits, characteristics, and underlying meanings.

But How Do I Know If I'm Accurate?

Chances are that even the very first time you attempt to analyze handwriting samples, some of your conclusions will be accurate, even if others are "off the mark." The more you practice, the more knowledgeable and accurate you will become.

A good way to gauge your accuracy is to work with a writing sample of someone you're casually acquainted with but don't know very well. Pick someone you think would be a "good sport" and reassure him or her that you're doing this for practice and fun.

Once you collect this sample and make your assessment, share it with the writer and have him or her tell you what you got right and what you might have missed. Then, go back over your worksheet, Chapter 2, and the Graphological Key to review. You should now have a better feel for this sample and reinforcement of your knowledge. Every experience builds confidence.

Trying Your Hand

It's now time for us to work together and get you in the graphological swing of things. Review the following writing sample and start creating a rough analysis, using the worksheet as a guide. Feel free to refer to sections in this book to help you along and reinforce what you know. Are you ready?

Handwriting Analysis Exercise

This is the writing of an eighty-one-year old, left-handed female.

Analysis

The first factor to determine is a high or low form level—this is a high form level based on the meticulousness, clarity, and organization on the page. For a left-handed woman, she has adapted well to a right-handed world, and the ease with which the letters are placed on the page shows that she uses her energies quite well.

This is a garland connection, which, as you recall, resembles an open cup. You will also see the rhythmic *e*'s, so typical of the garland writer, with which the writing was placed on the page.

You can also see the garland in the *n*'s and *m*'s. The garland connection tells you that this is a person who enjoys mediating, doesn't like conflict, and likes living things and nature. The writer allows for margins on both sides, which shows a sense of aesthetics, creating a frame for the picture of her writing. The pressure is light, which means that she may have some energy and vitality issues, based on her age; it also shows that she has sensitivity to others. We ask for age, as you would never guess that the writer is eighty-one.

The extension of the letters shows that she is focused and tries to deal with her emotions through logic. The size of the letters shows that she is precise and meticulous. She could have been a good schoolteacher, or she would have done well as an assistant to a CEO.

The letters are also school type, which shows that she was highly influenced by the way she was taught to write. This is a woman of integrity, as seen by the legibility and clarity of the writing—she has no secret agenda. The slant does go down a bit, which could be her age, i.e., feelings of fatigue.

The lower zone is the most pronounced on the page, and if you look at the word *renting*, which is on the third line of the sample, and the word *sharing*, which is on the sixth line of the sample, you will see that the lower zone extends quite a bit down the page but in a very graceful way, almost like a musical note. This could be a signal of her searching for answers to questions that have no answers. She does not bring the stroke of the lower zone back to the baseline, which could mean that there are certain things she would prefer not to know or bring to her conscious awareness.

This is the writing of a high-functioning person. There is regularity and consistency to it, which means that her performance is regular and consistent.

This writer is a feeling type who came from a conventional background. The clarity between the lines shows that she can listen and not impose herself on others. There is good spacing between the words as well.

I believe this is a person of loyalty, who is capable of great friendship, providing you play by the rules and do not unsettle her.

Getting to Know You

Now let's turn the tables and learn more about you! Wouldn't you like to see where the true you has been hiding all these years? Record your own writing sample for analysis so you can review it objectively and determine your strengths and weaknesses. This process will help you explore parts of your personality that you may not consciously be aware of or talents and aptitudes you might want to tap into. You'll also see how your handwriting is a reflection of your state of mind or mood at this very moment. This insight can be helpful in heading off potential issues before they become problematic.

PEN POINT   Handwriting, Moods, and Health

Each of us has innate qualities and aptitudes that remain consistent whenever we write. These qualities include our IQ, abilities, and temperament. However, other personal qualities are transient; they are changed by internal and external factors that can alter our writing from day to day. These factors include our health, attitudes, moods, stress, or energy levels. So, if you look at samples of your writing over a period of time, you'll understand more about why it might look a little different today than it did last month. Think back to what was going on around the time you wrote the last sample. Were you stressed or tired? Suffering from a migraine headache or indigestion? Angry with a partner or family member? Taking any prescription medication or sipping a cosmopolitan? These factors will affect your writing.

Let's start with you as you are today. On the following page, which we've purposely left blank, begin writing a short note with a ballpoint pen. If you'd prefer not to write in this book, get a clean, blank sheet of unlined paper, preferably 8½ by 11 inches. (Go ahead, we'll wait!)

Now, compose a short note to yourself. Don't get hung up on what you should write about—just keep it simple and let it flow. Write as much as you want, and if your thoughts take you through the whole page, so much the better. Once you're done, the revelations can begin.

A Fun and Revealing Project

Many people keep diaries and journals and photo albums of themselves through the years. You can also start and maintain a file of samples of your handwriting from your childhood up to the present day. Find old letters, school or work papers, diaries—anything that shows your handwriting, and your signatures, over the years. When you want to practice your newfound knowledge of graphology, start reviewing these samples. The results could be enlightening!

If you don't have access to written material from your past (or simply want to supplement the material you already have), create a file of writing samples from the coming weeks, months, or years. Feeling exhilarated after a wonderful evening with that special someone? Record your thoughts on paper. Home sick with the flu? Jot down your thoughts. Frustrated because your car has to go to the shop for yet another expensive repair? Write about that, too. In fact, every time you have a major event, illness, mood swing, or life frustration, make a conscious effort to write down a few paragraphs and place these pages in the file (remember to note the date). Before long you'll have a variety of your own samples to review. You'll be amazed at how your handwriting changes depending on your state of mind or health at any given moment.

PEN POINT   One Is Good, Two or More Is Better

As a rule, it is preferable to collect several samples from each person whose writing you'd like to analyze. Just as your own moods, health, and emotions change frequently, those of your subjects do too. When you have a selection of samples from the same person to review, you'll get a broader, more accurate picture of that person and what makes him or her tick.

CHAPTER 5

Looking for Mr. Write

*   *   *

HANDWRITING AND ROMANTIC COMPATIBILITY

Is this person your soul mate or just "one date"? Handwriting reveals emotional and psychological traits that lie beneath the surface of an outwardly warm and charming individual. Learn more about what makes a potential mate tick and whether or not you're romantically compatible. This chapter will examine various relationships within the context of handwriting and provide examples of notable couples (like Prince Charles and Princess Diana) to illustrate the pleasures and pitfalls of their relationships.

The cure for "love at first sight" is to take another look.

—MILTON BERLE

ASK ANY WOMAN about her search for true love and she will likely admit that she had to kiss a lot of "frogs" before finding a "prince." While it's true that with experience, maturity, and assorted heartaches, we eventually become wiser about who's right for us and who's not, the road to romance can be long and bumpy.

One of the wonderful ways graphology can help you is by giving a glimpse into the psyche and true character of whomever you're dating. During a courtship, we're generally so swept away by the attraction, excitement, and discovery of a new person that we're not inclined to examine what is lurking below the surface. It takes months, if not years, for someone's true personality, idiosyncrasies, or demons to emerge, and if our initial feelings or judgments have been misguided, we could be in for some heavy disappointment, frustration, and heartbreak.

No matter whom we fall in love with, if the relationship continues long enough, that initial euphoria subsides. The passion and ecstasy that characterize the initial period of falling in love always pass, and real life sets in. You discover, all too soon, that he wants sex, you don't. He wants to save money; you want to spend it. You want to talk about your job; he wants to talk about his. And so on. The truth is, no matter how much we desire or aspire to be "one" with someone else, our partner has and will always continue to have his own tastes, desires, prejudices, values, and priorities. The challenge of true love is to care enough to stay together and make compromises. Real love is a permanently self-enlarging experience in which we want to nurture another's development.

*   *   *

After a quarrel, a husband said to his wife, "You know, I was a fool when I married you. She replied, "Yes, dear, but I was in love and didn't notice."

—INTERNET JOKE

*   *   *

During the courtship period, everybody is on their "best behavior." We show our best sides to the other and they to us. Many an engagement or marriage is rushed into on the basis of a perception of a public persona that will change drastically with time and familiarity. When the veil has been lifted, it can be a rude awakening. And people can be quick to blame the relationship instead of their own unrealistic expectations.

Too often, we make untimely commitments to others because we are thinking with our hearts rather than our heads. After the flames of passion subside, often the person we thought was "the One" turns out to be just "another one." Ironically, we can readily see this coming in the relationships of others, but we're naïve about our own relationships.

While it's true that we should always trust our instincts about the people we let into our lives and our hearts, it's certainly worthwhile to consider a budding relationship from a more objective perspective, if only to confirm that our instincts are correct. By examining your handwriting in relationship to another's, you'll be able to see what you have in common—emotionally, intellectually, sexually, socially, and spiritually—and, more important, where you are likely to conflict. Besides, when you understand more about your differences, you'll be able to gauge whether these are issues on which you can compromise or adapt, or areas you can conquer together, or whether these matters are apt to pull you apart.

*   *   *

A woman marries a man hoping he'll change;
A man marries a woman hoping she won't.

—ANONYMOUS

*   *   *

Key Areas of Compatibility

In determining compatibility, graphology can provide a unique window into the mind, body, and spirit of another person. By having knowledge of someone's hidden agenda, you not only better understand the other, but see the ways you might click . . . or conflict.

Handwriting analysis can help you discover more in five key areas: emotional accessibility and intimacy, intellectual compatibility, sexual attraction, sociability, values and integrity.

Emotional Accessibility and Intimacy

Are you a talker and a feeler? Do you wear your heart on your sleeve? Can you show your vulnerability to another? Do you need someone who's as demonstrative in displaying affection as you are? If you have a fight, do you each forgive the other or do you or your partner hold a grudge? If you choose a mate who can't satisfy your emotional needs or provide you with intimacy, you could wind up feeling cheated and misunderstood. While an innately loving and affectionate person can defrost a cool, undemonstrative partner, the challenge is whether a partner's old wounds can reappear and create detachment or anger.

Here are some keys to emotional accessibility in handwriting:

- Regularity or fullness of letters
- Moderate pen pressure
- Balanced word and letter spacing
- Steady baseline
- Strong garland connection
- Right slant

Intellectual Compatibility

Though the movies are filled with heartwarming love stories about CEOs, millionaires, and scholars falling in love with call girls, chambermaids, or bowling alley waitresses, and walking off into the sunset together, we never get a glimpse of where those relationships go after the sun comes up. Much can be said about opposites attracting, but one's gray matter can prove to be a gray area when it comes to relationship longevity. Good relationships are mentally stimulating. If two people inspire each other's minds and creativity, then they can grow to be compatible intellectually.

Here are some keys to intellectual harmony in handwriting:

- Well-organized space
- Straight left margin
- Balanced or wide line spacing
- Small, legible writing
- Original and creative connections
- Sharp strokes
- Moderately to highly connected writing

- Right trend
- Normal pressure

Sexual Attraction

Are you and your partner physically compatible and attracted to each other? Are your sexual drives in sync? Can you accommodate each other's sexual appetites? And what if your paramour suddenly shows a dark side of offbeat fetishism or dysfunction? Could you have been forewarned?

Here are some keys to sexuality in handwriting:

- Pronounced loops in the lower zone
- Pastose strokes
- Pressure in the lower zone
- Strong pressure on the page
- Energy and vitality in connection

Sociability

Are you a social butterfly and your partner a homebody? How are your potential mate's interpersonal skills? Does he or she have lots of friends or acquaintances, or is your lover basically a loner? If you get into an argument, does one of you attack and the other retreat?

Here are some keys to sociability in handwriting:

- Consistently narrow right margin
- Narrow word spacing
- Balanced or wide letter spacing
- Strong middle zone
- Strong garland connection
- Moderately connected writing
- Right slant
- Active, lively rhythm

Values and Integrity

What are your goals and objectives? What are your partner's? What are your honesty and commitment levels to each other? Do you share moral codes and belief systems?

Here are some keys to positive values, honesty, and integrity in handwriting:

- Wide left margin and/or wide upper margin
- Developed upper zone
- Highly connected writing
- Upright slant
- Light to moderate pressure
- Legible letters
- Steady baseline
- Clarity of space
- Organized patterns
- Even discharge of ink
- Rhythmic style

Of course, there are many other aspects that might be of relevance, and you can be mindful of them as you undertake an analysis. It is also true that individuals may be compatible in some key areas but not in others. This is when knowing your differences can truly help you understand the potential pitfalls of your relationships and curtail friction before it starts.

Remember that graphology takes some time and effort to learn—it's like learning a new language. But as you're learning, allowing graphology to help you understand yourself and your relationship with others is one way you can directly experience this discipline. If you find yourself feeling overtly curious about a current relationship, consider consulting a professional graphologist or enroll in a graphology class to gain further insight.

PEN POINT   One Man's Poison Is Another Man's Pleasure

"Mr. Right" is not just elusive but also subjective! The truth is, someone your best friend thinks is fabulous might be someone you would never think of dating. That's why blind dates don't always work out—you're matched up with someone else's idea of a compatible mate for you. The people setting you two up may know only your superficial likes and interests, but if they don't know your respective "inner" personalities, the date is a one-shot deal.

Remember that person you first dated whom you were swept away by but could never pin down? You know the one—the type who couldn't make the kind of commitment you wanted, who had a roving eye and was charming and attractive to everyone (causing you to feel jealous)? Then one day you run into that person and find out he's a happily married family man, and you wonder, What did she have that I didn't to make him commit?

Many times, even if you believed that he was your Mr. Right, he didn't think you were right for him. So he eventually chose someone he sensed could better handle his drives and needs.

Who said relationships were easy?

Handwriting Clues for You to Use

Eighty percent of married men cheat in America. The rest cheat in Europe.

—Jackie Mason

Looking for a mate who's loyal? A good lover? An impressive wage earner? Someone with a sense of humor? And a good relationship with his family?

Here's a list of handwriting clues that'll help you know a little more about whom you're dating. Do realize that this is just a quick reference—to get to the real truth about another person, you will need to spend time studying his writing and, most of all, time with him.

Best Bets
Romeo the Romantic

- Organized space pattern
- Legible words
- Narrow word spacing
- Pastose strokes
- Diverse and creative connective forms
- Lots of movement
- Steady baseline

Gavin the Giver

- Garland connections
- Full or pastose strokes
- Accentuated middle zone
- Rightward slanting
- Uneven writing, but relaxed and flexible
- Light to average pressure
- Good and lively rhythm

Mr. Goodcatch

- Moderate pressure
- Original forms
- Clear writing and signature
- Large and wide writing
- Moderate rhythm

Questionable or Bad Bets
Larry the Ladies' Man

- Changing margins and wavy baseline
- Fast-paced writing

- Light pressure
- Unconnected letters
- Thread and angle connections
- Elaborate start to signature and embellished letters
- Uneven lines, rising

Seductive Sam

- Developed lower zone
- Pastose strokes
- Narrow word spacing
- Strong rightward movement
- Heavy pressure

(Watch out for quirks in the lower zone; unconventional *p*'s, *g*'s, or *y*'s could reflect a kinky sexual orientation!)

Lonnie the Loner

- Sharp, angular connections and strokes
- Small writing
- Wide word, line, and margin spacing
- Simplified style
- Narrow letters
- Descending lines

In Chapter 8, we'll explore in more detail the dishonorable and dark side of character in writing and show you how to spot warning signs.

He's Just My Type!

Another way to gauge whether someone might be your type is to determine his typology. As we saw in Chapter 3, there are six personality types, as defined by Carl Jung, which can be discovered in handwriting: extrovert, introvert, sensing, intuitive, thinking, and feeling. So, if you like a man who's the strong, silent type, you might prefer an introvert. Need someone more sensitive? Then see if he's a feeling type. Stimulated by a man with a brilliant mind? Chances are you'll be more compatible with a thinking type.

By assessing the typology in the handwriting of a potential partner, you'll get a good glimpse into his personality and how he would likely respond to you in a variety of social and personal situations.

A Look at Famous Couples

Throughout history, famous and infamous lovers have been of great public interest. Let's take a look at some well-known couples and see why their relationships have ended or endured. Although a great deal has been written about these couples, let us see how it is expressed in their handwriting.

FRIDA KAHLO AND DIEGO RIVERA:
Art Imitates Life

Frida Kahlo and Diego Rivera, famed artists who were the subject of a recent film, made an unlikely couple: she, physically petite and darkly exotic; he, corpulent and ugly. Together their lives were pure theater: written about in the press and watched in fascination by the bohemian art circles of the times.

Frida Kahlo

Abril 27- 1954
Salí sana - Hice la
promesa y la cumpliré
de jamás volver atrás.

Frida, a feeling type, was capable of living for something outside herself. In addition to it being highly creative, her writing is very passionate, possessive, and obsessive. The letters are pastose, the pattern is pleasure-oriented, and the uprightness shows her tremendous discipline and courage to rise above her afflictions. Frida was in a horrific bus accident and had been in constant emotional and physical pain since she was eighteen; she lived the rest of her life with an iron rod in her spine. She was obsessed with Diego, and as he became more deceitful toward her, she became more maternal toward him—to the point of bathing and caring for him as if he were a child.

There was nothing casual about this woman. She approached her life with passion and intensity. She had an extraordinary will to endure. You would never guess by the form level of this writing that it was written the last year of her life, when she was very ill. Instead, you see somebody who wanted to take as big a bite out of life as she could. She understood the nature of love, as seen by the spacing. Frida could be overwhelming, jealous, and possessive. With a strong temperament, she didn't take a backseat. She demanded a lot because she gave a lot. She could engulf a man unless he had his own strong identity. The large writing presses into the paper and floods it with abandonment, yet it is contained within the form, showing that she respected the boundaries of the page. She would throw herself into whatever situation she found herself in and, despite her frailty, was a woman of great vitality. You can see her life force on the page.

Frida's writing is very emotional: round, full-formed, lively, and quick, with a sense of beauty. However, lurking beneath these inflated forms are depression and feelings of emptiness. You can see this in the large loops, the rounded forms filled with feeling, and the poor navigation of space, which leaves little room for emotional clarity.

Diego's writing is free-flowing and full of creative juices, whereas Frida's is much more disciplined. It took great effort for her to execute this writing, with less speed than Diego, whose writing is easygoing and full of joie de vivre.

Diego, another feeling type, has a large middle zone—showing that he was a very self-involved, formal person, one who liked to take care of his own needs. Frida said two tragedies happened in

Diego Rivera

DIEGO

her life: the bus accident and meeting Diego. The bus accident happened once, whereas Diego was an accident happening over and over again. His misbehavior, self-involvement, and sense of entitlement are seen in the extremely large middle zone; his charm seen in the smoothness of execution, the quality of his garlands, and the easy flow toward the right. He knew what he wanted but found it difficult to make changes or adapt to another's needs because of his pursuit of his own satisfaction. And though he could be emotionally generous and compassionate at times, he tended to his own needs first.

Frida was a very needy person. Her overconnected writing shows that she forced herself to keep going. She had immense willpower. As a couple, however, neither would change: she was immovable, he was irresistible, and both were drawn to each other. She was impulsive and he was free-flowing. He appreciated her intelligence, aesthetic awareness, and depth of perception; she appreciated the same in him but wanted more commitment while Diego was first and foremost committed to himself.

JOANNE WOODWARD AND PAUL NEWMAN:
A Hollywood Success Story

When celebrities wed—especially in this day and age—it surprises no one if the union doesn't last past the first anniversary. But the marriage of Paul Newman and Joanne Woodward is an exception—it is one of the silver screen's most enduring relationships. Why do these two get along so well?

Joanne's writing is lively. There is considerable roundness and fullness in the garland connections, showing that she is nurturing and caring. Yet the writing is also very upright and slightly thready, which goes against the quality of the roundness. This is because she is very sensitive, and knowing that her sensitivity can render her vulnerable, she protects herself by maintaining a certain amount of personal control. The writing also threads into a diminuendo, with letters that start off large but get smaller. This shows she is very good at perceiving situations around her.

A combination of thinking and feeling types, Joanne is a highly intelligent woman, seen in her sophisticated letter connections. She is logical, orderly, and able to understand how things work. Her upright writing reveals her independence and need to do things her own way. She is flexible but can be resistant. She needs to be heard but presents herself in a gentle, graceful way.

Joanne has a high level of psychological understanding, seen in the impressive space patterns, which no doubt have helped her in being married to one of our most famous movie idols. Her warmth and support, coupled with discipline and independence, have helped her to complement her husband while maintaining her own identity.

Both Paul and Joanne are in touch with their feelings. Paul begins his first name with a huge capital *P*, which means he has the necessary narcissism of the actor, but the letter's simplicity reflects his intelligence. The thread connection reveals his creativity and unpredictability. His capitals show his need to present himself strongly to others. The *N* obliterates the rest of his last name with its size and scope. *Paul* is written more legibly, showing his pride in his accomplishments. Yet the paraph emphasizes his last name. The curl at the end of the word *wishes* goes into the lower zone, showing assertiveness and introspection. The writing, indicative of an intuitive typology, is quick and aggressive. The "Best wishes" is disconnected and impatient—this is a man who marches to the beat of his own drummer and is difficult to pin down. His need for excitement and stimulation is shown by his offbeat letter formations. He enjoys being an iconoclast who expects others to adapt to him. He needs a partner who has her own identity and can give him both his space and freedom, something Joanne is able to do. This possibly is a key reason why this couple has had a long, successful relationship.

ELIZABETH TAYLOR AND RICHARD BURTON:
Tabloid Twosome and True Love

Here's a relationship that anointed the permanent presence of the paparazzi. As you may know, during the shooting of the epic film *Cleopatra*, Elizabeth Taylor and Richard Burton became a steamy couple on screen and off (and both were married to others at the time). They divorced, married, divorced, remarried, and divorced again over the course of a decade, and Taylor, married eight times, still admits that Burton was the major love of her life. What can their writing tell us?

Despite this meager sample, one can see that Richard Burton was brilliant. He had a quick, thready, simplified writing style and a high degree of originality. The initial letters in his name are huge. This is a signal that he had ego insufficiency issues, which are compensated for by the oversize capitals. *Richard* is written with more clarity than *Burton*, which, you may recall, means that the writer is proud of his own achievements rather than those of his family (as the last name represents family ties).

Richard was most definitely a thinking type, and more intellectual and reflective than Elizabeth, who is dramatic, highly impulsive, ego driven, and sensation seeking. We would call Elizabeth's style an example of fast writing. Nothing is considered;

everything is quick and done for theatrical effect. She seems to live to the maxim "Nothing succeeds like excess."

Elizabeth Taylor, a feeling type (as you may recall from Chapter 3), writes without boundaries, and there is no stopping what she wants to do. The confusion with overlapping lines in her first and last names means that she is not interested in self-reflection, whereas Richard was highly introspective. Elizabeth prefers seduction by activity and the drama of her actions, the excitement of the moment.

The relationship between Elizabeth and Richard may have worked for as long as it did because they saw each other's strengths, weaknesses, and narcissistic needs gratified (as well as eventually rejected). Elizabeth often has difficulty in sensing the needs of another (except for short periods of time), whereas Richard often could, and she may have proven quite a handful for him. She is impulsive, while he was refined. Richard was attracted by beauty, drama, and royalty, and no doubt represented to Elizabeth the refinement and high intellect that she finds so impressive. Passion and excess, which Elizabeth's writing exemplifies, can burn themselves out over time and, like fire, they can warm a room or intensify wildly and become an inferno.

BILL AND HILLARY CLINTON:
Stain Resistant

Here's a relationship that surely defies the odds. Although this marriage has been examined for years in the media, let's see what compelling graphological clues we can find that explain why—amid one of the biggest scandals to befall an American president—Bill Clinton still stands and Hillary still stands by her man.

Former President Bill Clinton, a man of contradictions and conflicts, is clearly a leader. He is a feeling type, and his writing has lovely simplifications, indicating superior intelligence. Notice the creative, original connections in the letters *th* in the words *thanks* and *they.* The variety in the *i* dots and the intelligent arrangement of space reveal a bright, clever person who loves challenges and the chance to impose himself on the world around him. (Note the circles on the sample of Clinton emphasize the letters being discussed. They are not in the original sample.)

As seen by the height of the upper zone, Bill derives pleasure from using his mind. Nevertheless, the writing reveals a powerful struggle between the need to achieve goals and assert himself, and the desire to placate and please others. Sometimes this conflict

BILL CLINTON

causes him to lose heart or confidence and to withdraw emotionally. But, strategic in his thinking, he eventually regroups and redefines himself to accomplish what he ultimately wants. The rounded fullness of the writing shows his amiability. The angularity signals his determination. The angles can be seen in *I'm* in the words *I'm grateful* and in *I welcome* and the words *they will.*

Bill appears soft, but there's more aggression underneath than is readily visible, as seen in the fullness and the size of the lower zone. Sometimes he has a short fuse, indicated by the spikiness in the writing.

Bill has a high energy level and enjoys using his senses. This is a pastose writing, meaning that he is always struggling with his self-indulgent tendencies. However, he has disciplined himself to be more effective. This discipline shows also in the uprightness of the writing and the openness of the letters. The overblown *B* in the signature is narcissistic. He can get too involved in his own agenda and may not really listen to others. Similarly, the signature at the bottom shows some hastiness and sloppiness. He is sometimes conflicted about achieving goals at others' expense, and that can hamper his decision making.

and support. With your help and support, we'll have a great victory on November 3rd. Best wishes — Hillary.

Hillary's mind-set can be described as masculine, while Bill's is feminine (which is a compliment). Whereas Bill is emotional, Hillary is not, so here, too, they complement each other.

Hillary, a thinking type, is cool. Her writing reflects a lot of pride—look at the size of the *H* in *Hillary.* In contrast, Bill is a smooth political animal. Hillary's brilliance is seen in the simplification of her letterforms and their speed, clarity, and originality.

The thread connection shows that she knows how to achieve her objectives. However, there is a dark side to the writing: she can manipulate to achieve personal power.

Given these psychological profiles, what drew Bill to Hillary and vice versa? I believe it was her exceptional intelligence. The simplicity and fluidity in Hillary's writing show insight, quickness, and discipline that enable her to cut through the nonessentials.

The Clintons' compatibility is based on their joint effectiveness. Each offers the other something of value. In other words, they increase their mutual as well as individual ambitions through their relationship. Regardless of the scandals and pitfalls that have besieged them, they have a true partnership in that Bill gives Hillary a tremendous amount of respect and deference. He respects her opinion and insight. She loves the ability to influence policy and people that he permits her. She has also learned to handle public situations very well despite the fact that she can be direct and disdainful, and that she hates games. She has learned to think less like a litigator and more like a politician.

The Clintons' compatibility lies in a shared commitment to common goals.

PRINCESS DIANA AND PRINCE CHARLES:
Unhappily Ever After

The *Newsweek* writer and television journalist Roger Rosenblatt described Diana this way: "She was the image every child has of a Princess—the kind who can feel the pea under the mattress, who kisses the frog, who lets her hair down from the tower window. Exactly how her life would have progressed is hard to imagine. No matter how old she might have become, her eyes would still have that sweet mixture of kindness and longing."

The letters in Diana's writing sample are rounded and full, relating to the pleasures of the mouth, such as enjoyment of food, which also represents comfort and a need to communicate, particularly on an emotional level. This oral roundness and fullness shows self-indulgence as well as a tendency toward melancholy. There is no question that Diana personifies a feeling typology.

(Circles were added for illustration of a point in this sample of Princess Diana.)

The left side of the page represents the mother or search for a mother. We note that the lower zone of Diana's *y*'s" moves to the left. The rounded, highly connected letters and narrow spaces between the lines show a need to reach out to others and be involved with them.

There is a charming, almost childlike quality to the pattern on the page, which reflects the writer's need to be reassured. There is warmth and sensitivity in the writing pattern and pressure. The letters are tightly written yet full, signifying emotional inhibitions. Diana was ambivalent about love: she searched for it but feared it at the same time. When this type of conflict exists, one turns to substitutes that are "safer." A person can easily become dependent on a substance or a feeling in order to feel "full." Food, shopping, or partying often fills this vacuum. In Diana's case, it was also sublimated by her involvement with charitable activities.

Diana's use of space is good. She presented herself smoothly and functioned well publicly, moving effectively through the space on the page. However, there is considerable emotional tension in the writing. The variety of the letters shows that she did not have proper

release for her feelings, that she could be easily wounded and somewhat unpredictable. This exquisite sensitivity helped her remain
childlike and trusting, and enabled her to relate well to her children.
Diana's writing is highly maternal—rounded and sensitive. She was
gifted in being able to give her children what she herself never had.

Notice the word *hope* in the fourth line down. There is no upper
zone and not much of a lower zone. The lack of an upper zone
shows a disregard for authority (and we all know that Diana was always in conflict with her powerful in-laws). The lack of a lower zone
represents a person who does not invite self-examination.

Diana's need to connect with others is also manifested by her
love of glamour and money. Look at the word *thoughts* in the
third line down, where the *g* goes into the lower zone and, instead
of returning to the baseline, punctuates the middle zone, inter-
rupting it. This signals a confusion of priorities.

The letters in the middle zone are large, but we can see a contra-
diction here: usually, letters that slant to the right indicate an extreme
emotional nature. However, the letters in Diana's middle zone are
upright, which shows she was working hard at restraint and self-
control. The rigidity and uprightness of the letters also show that she
could be compulsive. The tug-of-war between her emotional needi-
ness and her desire for restraint was one of the dramas of her private
life, manifesting itself in her intense need for human contact.

The clarity of the space attests to her idealism and search for
causes. The personal pronoun *I* is no larger than the rest of this
heavily middle-zoned writing. The largest letter on the page is the
D in *Diana,* which is sophisticated and elegant. No doubt, the signature was practiced.

In contrast, Prince Charles's writing is tighter, dryer, and more
crablike. Charles is both a thinking typology and an introvert.
Diana was more comfortable in the limelight than her husband was.

In Charles's writing there is considerably more distance between
words, letters, and lines than in Diana's sample. This shows his fear
of intimacy: he is a man who lives within himself. Diana was fueled
by stimuli from the outside. Charles's writing has a left trend or
slant (even though he is right-handed), indicating introspection. The
line under Charles's name, unlike that under Diana's, has a hook,

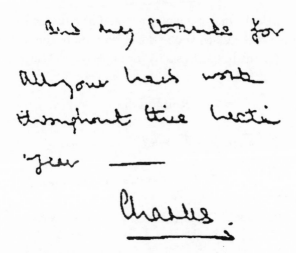

which indicates tenacity. The sparseness of the writing pattern also confirms the prince's difficulty in reaching out emotionally.

The space between the lines in Charles's writing is clear, and the letters are simplified, indicating considerable intelligence. No doubt Charles saw Diana as childish and impulsive, as well as indulgent and needy. She, in turn, viewed him as remote, judgmental, and cerebral. Diana, who lacked formal education, did not have strong intellectual skills and relied heavily on her emotions.

Communication between them was difficult. Diana was chosen by Charles to be his wife because of her bloodline, youth, shy demeanor, and virtuousness, but these were superficial qualities on which to build a lasting marriage. As we know, the couple could never be soul mates, and their union suffered as a result.

Mr. Right or Mr. Wrong?

A Compatibility Quiz

I married Mr. Right. I just didn't know his first name was "Always."

—Anonymous

How well do you think you know another person? Here's a test. Review these three handwriting samples, do a brief analysis of each, then circle the one of the person you'd be most inclined to have a relationship with. When you're done, learn more about the person you chose. You might be pleasantly (or unpleasantly) surprised!

Round One

1.

> TO WHOM IT MAY CONCERN
>
> FIRST EVERYONE UNDER
> NOTHING TO DO WITH
> I Loved HER, ALLWAYS.
> ALWAYS WILL. IF WE HAD A
> ITS BECAUSE I Loved HER So
> RECITLY WE CAME TO the UNDR
> THAT (FOR) NOW WE WENT RIG
> EACH OTHER AT LEAST FOR NOW.
> OUR LIFE WE WERE DIFFERENT
> THATS WHY WE MUTUALLY AGRe
> (GO OUR SEPARATE WAYS. IT
> TOUGH SPITTING FOR A SECOND
> BUT WE BOTH KNOW IT WAS FOR
> BEST. INSIDE I HAD NO DOUB
> IN THE FUTURE WE WOULD BE
> AS FRIEND OR MORE.
>
> UNLIKE WHATS BEEN IN
> PRESS, NICOLE - I HAD A GREAT
> FOR MOST OF OUR Lives TOGETHE
> ALL LONG TERM RELATIONSHIP WE
> FEW DOWNS + UPS. I TOOK THE
> YEARS 1989 BECAUSE THAT WHAT
> SUPPOSE TO DO I DID NOT
> FOR ANY OTHER REASON BUT TO
> PRIVACY AND WAS ADVISE IT WOULD
> PRESS HYPE KNOCKING I DON'T
> BELABOR KNOCK. THE

2.

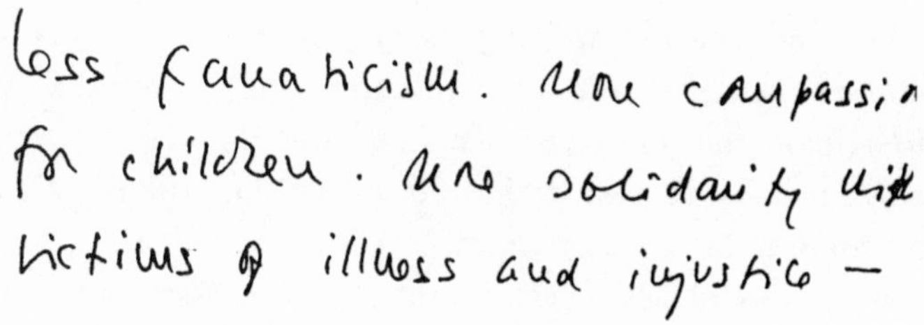

> *less fanaticism. more compassion for children. more solidarity with victims of illness and injustice —*

3.

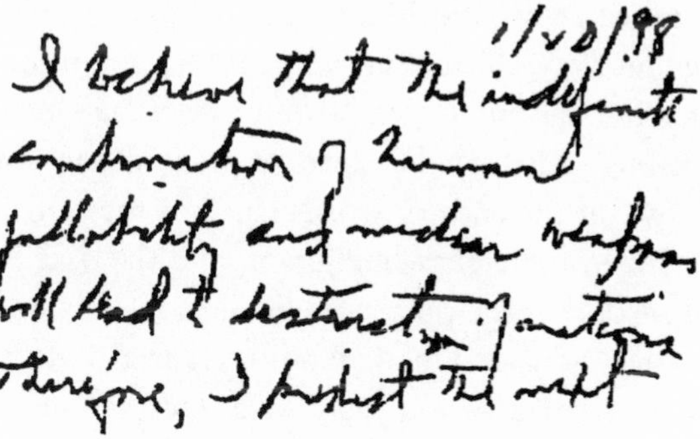

> *[handwritten, largely illegible]* 11/20/98
> *I believe that the indefinite combination of human fallibility and nuclear weapons will lead to destruction of our species. Therefore, I predict the end ...*

Write the number of the man you would most like
to date here. _____

Descriptions Revealed

1. *O. J. Simpson* If you find this a writing of someone you would like to know better, you have chosen one of the most controversial men of the 1990s, O. J. Simpson!

    Although written while under extreme duress and potentially exaggerated, even at first glance this writing displays powerful emotions and mood swings. See how the word *whom* in the first line dips below the ruled line? Even though the lined paper provides a concrete guide, he ignored it. Instead, the writing moves in a wavy pattern, showing an inability to control his feelings. O. J. is pulled by contradictory emotions, shown in the mixture of left- and right-slanted letters (for example, in the fourth line: "I loved her, allways"). A person whose love is stable and dependable doesn't demonstrate such conflict of feelings.

Throughout his writing O. J., an intuitive typology, combines upper- and lowercase printing, as in the word *different* in the tenth line. This signifies that he has trouble distinguishing between right and wrong. His values can shift according to his need or whim.

In various places in the sample, O. J. crosses out a word using multiple strokes, making it black with pressure. This means that he can't be told he's wrong or take criticism. He wants things his way, no matter what. Pressure him or point out any of his failings and anger, hostility, even rage may erupt without warning. This quality also is seen in the way the letters get larger at the ends of words (such as the *r* at the end of the word *for* in the eighth line down, and the *d* at the end of the word *second* in the thirteenth line), as well as multiple-size letters. They indicate a man who is mercurial, emotionally erratic, and potentially explosive. In fact, some of the punctuation marks, such as the intense period at the end of the first paragraph, suggest a sadistic tendency.

Printing is often used to mask one's real identity; it gives a pleasing presentation and suggests emotional control. The fact that O. J. prints instead of using script explains why people rarely see him for what his ex-wife knew him to be.

The writing is fluid, and the letterforms display an above-average intelligence. The space between words, while somewhat uneven, is basically pleasing. This space picture reveals a man who knows his way around. Inner conflicts, as reflected in the handwriting, are those of a troubled, unfulfilled, and unstable private person.

2. *Elie Wiesel*   This is a man with the most refined sensibilities, whose writing style is intelligent, as seen in the highly original letter and garland forms. It is Nobel Prize winner Elie Wiesel. He is both a feeling and a thinking type. His range of sensitivity to living things and ability to identify with other people's emotions are seen throughout his writing. This is a highly compassionate person with a profound inner

awareness. He is willing to make a deep and honorable commitment and has high ideals, shown in the clarity and openness of the writing, as well as the delicacy of the letters. The wide spaces are a testament to his active inner life. He has a developed, feminine polarity. He can intuit the needs of others, particularly a partner, so there can be a good, nourishing emotional exchange between them. He needs a partner who is both cultivated and well developed, who can give him validation and protect him and his solitude. He needs a partner with similar ideals, who is more of an extrovert and will take care of the details of life so he can stay in the world of the mind. He is immersed in his own ideas and is creative, sensitive, and self-involved. In the word *children,* the *d* with the *i* connection shows his brilliance and simplification.

The way the *f* forms the first stroke of the *o* in the word *for* is another marvelous simplification. A lot of words are split, which may represent conflicts within himself. Wiesel's upper zone is low, making this middle-zone writing.

Like a rare orchid, Wiesel needs space and care. If treated in this way, he will reward his partner many times over.

3. *Robert McNamara*   This sample is by Robert McNamara, secretary of defense under President Kennedy and President Johnson, who was an intuitive and smart man. The high upper zone of his writing shows that he behaves quite individualistically. His legible writing is a combination of angle and thread, which confirms his intellect.

People with this writing style want to do what they want when they want, and in their own style. McNamara does not want to be limited. He is extraordinarily intelligent, sharp in his perceptions, as seen in the interesting high connections, but he does what is politic and expedient, so in a relationship he may be wont to have the other adjust to his needs. The connections, thread, and angle may cause one to be wary in a relationship with him.

Round 2

1. That all people
will be free!

2. I predict there
will be auto racing
on Mars before
the year 3000.

3. I try to live by the Golden
Rule — — to always accord
others the same dignity,
decency, and respect that
we all want in our own
lives. In my experience,
you can achieve much
more by bringing others
along with you.

Write the number of the man you would most like
to date here. _____

Descriptions Revealed

1. *Oliver North*   This is the writing of Oliver North, a decorated Marine Corps veteran in the Vietnam War, who became famous for his involvement in the Iran-Contra scandal. North, an intuitive, uses huge letters in his writing, which means he needs to have a partner who can support his ego and self-image. He is a bright man, more introverted than he appears. All the letters are very close together, showing a lot of inhibition. He is a person of mixed qualities, and a partner has to be able to support and understand this sensitive, inhibited side, as well as to participate and be the loyal soldier to the appearance of the extroverted side.

2. *Mario Andretti*   If you chose this person, you chose someone who really lives life in the fast lane—the racing car driver Mario Andretti. Clarity and detail can be seen in the separation of the letters, which he carries over into whatever he does. There is a disconnection as well, which shows a concern about exactitude. Andretti, an intuitive, prints everything individually and in sequence, and does it precisely. The lower zone has an angle in it, indicating that he is pretty competitive. He has "an idea in place," and his partner must understand that and work within the limitations he imposes. Andretti is not a man who will give repeated reassurances and recognition to his companion.

3. *Richard Gephardt*   If you selected this sample, you've picked Richard Gephardt, Democratic leader in the U.S. Congress. Gephardt's script reveals a conventional and conservative upbringing, but the writing is very connected, which shows his logic and ability to make what he is doing work for a purpose. The writing moves toward the right, and there is a strong right trend, indicating that he is moving toward his goals. Gephardt has just enough thread that he is able to make the adjustments and do the politicking necessary in his career. He is a natural-born conciliator who has well-defined ideals and a great deal of clarity in his writing. He is well organized and careful about not interfering in the space on the page.

A feeling type, Gephardt is a dependable, consistent, and decent man. He needs someone who can nurture and support him to realize his goals, one who is respectful of the limitations his value system has imposed on him. He is not going to do things that are unconventional or violate the values and principles of his past.

Round Three

1. You have achieved excellence as a leader when people will follow you anywhere, if only out of curiosity

2. The real heroes are men and women who are friends of the poorest of the poor.

3. I hope the millennium will finally bring us a nuclear free world!

Write the number of the man you would most like to date here. _____

Descriptions Revealed

1. *Colin Powell* This sample belongs to Secretary of State Colin Powell. You can see his fear of making mistakes and being disliked through the right slant of his handwriting. His movement to the right means he has learned how to behave as an extrovert.

   The wide spaces between words show that Powell keeps his own counsel. The writing is clear and legible, revealing that he is a perfectionist. The printing is a mixture of upper- and lowercase, which shows his maneuverability and his desire to adjust.

   The slant leans too far to the right for print—in most printed writing, there is an upright slant. Because of the mixing of upper- and lowercase block letters we can conclude that this represents a fundamental uncertainty of feelings. Powell is a conciliatory general, not a creative or visionary one. His purpose is to mediate and build consensus, to which he is temperamentally better suited.

   His writing has a strong emphasis on the upper zone. He is an idealistic and ambitious man, careful to make every letter separate. There is a certain calculation in his decision making, which shows caution and concern for consequences. Powell is intelligent enough to organize the space well, and his clarity of thinking is seen throughout. He needs a wife to provide emotional stability but does not need a lot of nurturing. His partner will provide the setting and conditions, as well as the space, so that he can thrive and accomplish his goals.

2. *Nelson Mandela* If you selected this writing, you've picked Nelson Mandela, the extraordinary South African leader. Mandela is a very emotionally centered person with a garland connection in his writing, seen particularly in the letters *m* and *n*. This shows his warmth and deep feeling. The clarity of the writing suggests his idealism, one who is very definite but is also sensitive to others, which is confirmed once more by the garland connection and fullness of the letters in the writing sample.

It is interesting that Mandela, certainly a feeling type, has this emotional sensitivity to others while at the same time being capable of stifling a civil war and trying to find resolution and forgiveness of those who have offended his race. He requires a partner who is both supportive and strong, sure enough in her own identity to understand his vision. There are details and responsibilities he finds annoying, and he needs to be relieved of this minutiae. Mandela needs a close partner because support and mutuality give him a sense of completion. The feminine polarity in his writing is strongly marked by both the roundedness of the letters and their articulation, which show him to be an empathic and receptive person. This can only represent a rewarding and responsive communication with his partner.

3. *Michael Douglas*   If you chose this man to date, you'd be going out with the actor-producer Michael Douglas. His writing shows that he has difficulty with impulse control, seen in the thread connection, variation in size of letters, and variation in slant. Douglas's writing is unconventional and individualistic, revealing that he doesn't obey the rules and must do things his own way.

Douglas is an intuitive typology. The writing pattern is all over the place, signifying a need for attention. The baseline is extremely variable, showing his mood changes. He is not an easy person to be with.

If you are strong enough to have your own sense of self, without constant need for reassurance, you will have a chance with Douglas, but this is not a relationship for the fainthearted! Douglas is charming. The variation in the form of the letters shows creativity and an unconventional streak, which makes him interesting. He is experimental, and that makes him exciting. However, the lack of consistency, the irregularity and the threadiness in the writing show his tendency toward self-indulgence and emotional immaturity.

Are You the One for Him?

As a final note, while you're on the quest for your Mr. Right, be mindful of what type of woman he might want and need. If you think about many of the famous men profiled in this chapter, you'll notice that those who are most driven and complex need certain types of women in order to have a lasting relationship. Most of these men want counterparts who will permit them to live out their agendas. Possessive, controlling, or needy women will present a problem. Other types of men might, instead, be searching for a woman who is more maternal, someone who nurtures and motivates them, someone who can take care of them or even take charge.

In pursuit of your dream relationship, be honest about the type of person you are and whether you can complement your partner's needs. While it will be disappointing to discover that you might not be the best match, it is better to be aware of this now, before you invest too much time and emotion. And if you want to know more about yourself, then look to your own handwriting (as explained in Chapter 4) for the answers.

CHAPTER 6

Are We on the Same Page?

* * *

BUSINESS RELATIONSHIPS

*Getting along with colleagues, whether partners,
employees, or co-workers, is key to making work life
productive, stimulating, and enjoyable. Does your boss have
a hidden agenda? Which person on your staff is worth promoting?
Which colleagues are team players who support you, and which
ones are potential opportunists or backstabbers? Graphology
can be a positive tool in improving business communications
and relationships, resolving conflicts, avoiding confrontations,
negotiating better deals, and helping you get an edge in your
career. Samples and signatures in this chapter will
uncover the dynamics between people and show
leadership traits in a variety of known movers
and shakers, including Donald Trump
and Bill Gates.*

*The secret of business is knowing something that nobody
else knows.*

—ARISTOTLE ONASSIS

WORK. It's where you spend the bulk of your day, your week, and
your life. If ever there was an environment in which you have to
strive to get along with everyone around you, this is it. Some
people you'll click with, and others you won't. And when you

don't, more time is spent focusing on relationship issues, gossip, or office politics than on productivity.

Friends we choose; families we're born into and grow up with; but when it comes to our business colleagues, they're an inherited mixed bag.

First, there's your boss (unless, of course, you're lucky enough to own your own business or be self-employed). Here is someone you truly want to please and who will, you hope, like and respect you. Do you really know what he or she expects from you? Is this someone who values your contributions? Do you know what makes your boss tick?

Second, there are your colleagues. How well do you know them? Are they simply people with whom you work and exchange superficial chitchat? Or are these people you like, trust, and look up to? These are people who, if you're fortunate, can make your job pleasurable and, if you're not, dull or difficult. Ideally, colleagues provide cooperation, partnership, brainstorming, support, and most of all, a bit of camaraderie.

And finally, if you're a manager, there is your staff. Though you might have a sense of the ones who are hard and dedicated workers by the tasks they complete and their attitudes on the job, are they employees worth promoting? Do you know who's a team player versus an instigator? Is there someone on your staff who aspires (or even conspires) to take your job? Keeping, hiring, or even firing an employee can also be a challenge. Is there a way to know who's the best person for a position?

Graphology can provide insight into the different types of people with whom you work and which ones you're most apt to respect and get on with. Intelligence, dedication, loyalty, self-motivation, sociability—these are valuable traits for business success. In fact, many corporations and business owners retain the services of professional graphologists to help them determine who has what it takes to succeed. Often good employees lose productivity when they're handling the wrong assignments, placed in the wrong department, or work among colleagues with whom they are not compatible. But with the knowledge that graphology reveals, supervisors are able to find ways to restructure or even streamline personnel to make everyone in a department or office work more effectively and efficiently.

By the way, if you are sincerely interested in how graphology can give you insight into your business or employees, you should consider hiring a professional graphologist rather than attempting this on your own. Until you've devoted several years to perfecting your knowledge of handwriting analysis, you would not want to risk making a mistake that might put your business—and credibility—at risk. Consult with a professional first. (See the end of Chapter 10 for more details.)

PEN POINT   Samples at Work: How Do You Obtain Them?

Obtaining writing samples at work is a sensitive subject—we don't want you to turn into the office snoop or get in any kind of trouble! The best way is to be as aboveboard as you can. First, see what you already have access to. Look at notes you've received from colleagues and employees, comments on a report, or signatures on expense reports, requisition forms, or letters.

The second option is simple: ask! Tell people you're studying handwriting analysis and would love to practice your craft. Colleagues in particular are likely to comply, provided you tell them a bit about what their handwriting reveals (try to be as upbeat and tactful as possible or simply tell them that you're still learning and want to learn more before you share your observations).

The third option is to be honest with people you know who can share these samples with you.

Finally, it's all right to be creative in your pursuit, but always be honest. Who knows? One day, when you really perfect your skills, your boss might seek out your graphological wisdom to help, along with other forms of asessments, make better choices for hiring.

Who's Really Who at the Office?
Eight Business Personalities

A good way to learn about your boss, employees, or co-workers is to understand that people usually fall into one of eight types of business personalities. As we learned in Chapter 3, examining common traits among personality types is useful for getting a basic, overall first impression of a person. In the business world, knowing your boss's, colleagues', or employees' work styles through their handwriting will also give you an initial, basic picture of their personalities.

Let's take a look at each of these personalities and their handwriting traits, so that you will recognize and learn how to better deal with them in your workplace.

The Mover and Shaker

The Mover and Shaker's goal is to attain power. Movers and Shakers experience life and work as a battle to be won. Most of their psychological resources are deployed for their internal department of defense. Movers and Shakers tend to see their peers as either accomplices or enemies, and their employees or subordinates as lieutenants to be utilized.

Movers and Shakers have historically been entrepreneurs and empire builders. Yet, despite power and material success, they are less likely to enjoy life the way average people do. In their quest for power, Movers and Shakers often have difficult relationships resulting in detrimental effects on their spouses and children.

While other personality types deeply dislike having to reprimand or fire anyone, Movers and Shakers take pride in wielding their power and in instilling fear. They believe that fear is a powerful motivator. Imposing fear also reinforces their feeling of control.

Here are the traits to look for in the writing of a Mover and Shaker:

- Angular and/or angular-thread connection
- Pressure

- Vitality and movement
- Speed
- Signature with large capitals
- Need for space
- Often illegible writing

Movers and Shakers include Aristotle Onassis, Michael Eisner, Donald Trump, Ron Perelman, Andrew Carnegie, John D. Rockefeller, and J. P. Morgan.

A Portrait of a Mover and Shaker:
DONALD TRUMP

THANKS FOR THE
MEETING — YOU ARE
REALLY GREAT AND I
LOOK FORWARD TO
WORKING WITH YOU
FOR MANY YEARS
TO COME —
Best Wishes
Donald

What's the first thing you notice when you look at this writing? The extreme angularity, of course! Real estate tycoon Donald Trump doesn't care what others think. The angularity is seen quite graphically in his signature and in the *n* in the first word, *thanks*, the *m* of the word *meeting* in the second line, the *n* in the word *and* in the third line, the *m* in the word *many* in the third line from the bottom, and the word *come,* the last word in the sentence. His level of aggression and ambition is so high that he is willing to override others' objections to achieve his goals.

Trump's is a tremendously driven, active, intense, forceful, goal-oriented writing. He likes control and needs to keep proving himself, but the angles in his writing show his impatience, intolerance, and inability to adapt. They also suggest that he will exclude anyone from his orbit who won't conform to his demands. Trump is unconcerned with the opinions of others.

Yet, despite the angles, which we often think of as rigidity, Trump is very resilient, as we can see in the tremendous drive and energy in the pressure of his writing. Nothing will keep this man down for long.

Notice that his writing is all in the middle zone, which represents the ego. His extreme angles and the spikiness of his letters—particularly his signature—show that there's room for only one person behind the barbed-wire fortress he's built—and that person is himself! You could say Trump has an edifice complex!

Like the man himself, Trump's signature is highly original, and because of its size, you can see his need to impose himself on the page that signifies his environment. Both tactical and strategic in his thinking, he is able to rally people to help him but remains very self-involved, as seen by the size of his middle zone.

Getting Along with a Mover and Shaker

If you work for *a Mover and Shaker . . .* find out what his or her expectations are and try your best to meet them. Movers and Shakers are often obsessive, so it pays to be focused and goal-oriented. They expect you to adjust to them, so it is important to do your due diligence and find out as much as you can about them and their needs. Ask questions, do research, and listen carefully. Document your successes—they may be helpful in a future negotiation.

Stay on the cutting edge of your field. You are there to make Movers and Shakers look good! Be prepared to have more than one plan of action. Stay in good physical shape, because Movers and Shakers can burn you out. Do not expect recognition from them because they are slow to give it. Ask for more responsibilities—the more you do, the more valuable a resource you'll become.

Working for a Mover and Shaker is not for the fainthearted! You'll encounter many surprises and inconsistencies. It is easy to become competitive with a Mover and Shaker, and this is a trap you should not fall into. Be prepared to feel somewhat used, because most Movers and Shakers are exploiters. Movers and Shakers are exciting and charismatic people, who love the adrenaline rush they get from taking risks, and take others along for the ride.

If you work with *a Mover and Shaker* . . . do not attempt friendship. It is more important that Movers and Shakers respect you than like you. If they sense you need approval, they will play on this need as a weakness.

If you supervise *a Mover and Shaker* . . . play to his or her strengths. What does this employee enjoy doing the most? What does he or she do best? Let Movers and Shakers use their ambition in ways that benefit both of you. If they are good at generating important connections and contacts for you or your business, encourage them to do so! Don't be judgmental, because they cannot be changed, nor do they want to be reined in. Instead, make them feel valuable and empowered and continue to challenge them— they will thrive on it.

The Firecracker

Firecrackers tend to be suspicious or distrustful of others. This trait is generally a carryover from youth, when they feared or lost faith in authority figures or anyone who had power over them. They frequently have difficulty taking a stand and question the views and motives of others. Firecrackers assuage their insecurity by seeking a protector or rebelling against authority. At their most extreme, Firecrackers can explode when confronted with conflict or the unexpected. They can be easily provoked. Their "internal theater" is filled with memories and demons from the past, which can be unexpectedly ignited.

Here are the traits to look for in the writing of a Firecracker:

- Intense pressure
- Variable baseline
- Uneven spacing and disorganized or unconventional space patterns
- Short endings to words
- Often pastose letters
- Poor spatial judgment
- Poor rhythm
- Unusual letter formations
- Angular connection

Examples of Firecrackers include O. J. Simpson, Fidel Castro, and Ted Turner.

A Portrait of a Firecracker:
TED TURNER

(This signature may appear different from his official one. It was written during a book signing.)

It's been rumored that on the desk of Ted Turner, broadcasting pioneer and founder of Cable News Network, there once was a sign that said, "Either lead, follow, or get out of the way." Through his evident belief in that direction, it's obvious that Turner exemplifies the Firecracker personality.

Turner's writing is large, signifying that he's an extrovert who craves attention. His writing, like his personality, goes to extremes. The *T* in *Ted,* the *T* in *Turner,* and the *r,* which is the last letter in his signature, all dip down into the lower zone, where they do not belong. The lower zone signifies our primal needs, material comforts, and a search for roots.

The tightness and tangled lines of Turner's signature reflect his intensity and competitiveness. See how the huge letters veer in different directions? This mirrors his mood swings and insecurity. Mood swings are also confirmed by the wavy baseline.

Turner creates his own letter formations, which have nothing to do with the traditional alphabet. At the top of some of his letters are fishhooks, which resemble a longshoreman's grafting hook. These show tenacity.

Turner's illegible writing indicates that he refuses to reveal his hand and conceals his real motives. He likes to keep others off balance. You never know what he is up to.

The movement in his writing is like a coil about to spring. He is capable of multiple agendas that can change quickly. A man of many interests, he also disposes of relationships quickly since his attention span is short. He hates authority, so he has no choice but to become the authority.

Getting Along with a Firecracker

If you work for *a Firecracker* . . . it can be trying, unless you are very secure. Firecrackers need reassurance and expect competence, loyalty, and obedience. Have your résumé ready because Firecrackers are volatile and often incapable of appreciation— their standards are so high, silence is often a sign of appreciation.

If you work with *a Firecracker* . . . you must have low expectations and realize that Firecrackers have a limited concept of loyalty. They are ruled by their feelings and have an enormous need for activity. Firecrackers can be restless and emotionally unreliable. Temper your expectations. It is best to try to be independent of Firecrackers, professionally and emotionally.

If you supervise *a Firecracker* . . . get out the Maalox! Firecrackers need structure, boundaries, and reassurance. They bring baggage from the past and require patience and evenhandedness. They rebel against authority and will always try to test your patience.

The Superstar

Superstars are adaptable, success-oriented types, who are self-assured, attractive, charming, ambitious, and energetic. They can also be competitive, driven, and image-conscious. Presenting a polished persona to the outside world, they seek attention and admiration, which in turn can lead them to become arrogant and opportunistic. Superstars are typically self-made people who often come from broken homes and tend to have poor family relationships. Keenly interested in the motives of others, they crave love and attention, but paradoxically, also want to be left alone.

Here are the traits to look for in the writing of a Superstar:

- Creative, innovative letters
- Good rhythm and speed
- Often large letters at the beginnings of words and in signatures
- Need for space
- Clarity of space between words and lines
- Good organization of space
- Moderate pressure
- Some illegibility

Examples of Superstars are: Warren Buffett, Greg Norman, Barbara Walters, Colin Powell, Oprah Winfrey, Tony Blair, and Bill Gates.

A Portrait of a Superstar:
BILL GATES

To my fellow Capitalist!
Thanks for coming?
Bill Gates

For a man whose success is virtually unparalleled, Bill Gates, CEO of Microsoft, has very "human" writing. He knows what he wants and how to nurture others who can help him achieve his goals. Maybe that's why industry experts rave about Microsoft's hiring practices. Gates's meticulous, well-connected letters show he leaves nothing to chance.

Gates's writing is fluid, with good rhythm and ease across the page. His ambition is evident in the strong movement toward the right, which also signifies reaching out to goals, challenges, and the future. Competitive and driven, his letters are connected, indicating focus, drive, and momentum. The speed, movement, simplicity of letter formations, clarity, and legibility of the letters emphasize strong two-way communication.

It is interesting that Gates's signature lacks the flamboyance associated with most entrepreneurs. However, the right slant underscores his perseverance and determination. And despite the speed of his thinking, Gates's clear writing shows that he wants to be understood by others.

Notice the way he forms the *G* in *Gates*. The stroke of the *G* becomes the top of the *a*, then he retraces the *a* tightly, closing it off. This is another sign that Gates needs to be in control.

Although he is often perceived as arrogant, Gates is actually determined, self-confident, and impatient. He expects that others be on par with his competence and intelligence.

Although he is left-handed, his writing moves to the right. The right slant reveals a need to reach out to others, to engage and enlist them in his projects. His large capitals show pride in achievement, and the overall large writing pattern dominating the page emphasizes his need for control.

Getting Along with a Superstar

If you work for *a Superstar* . . . you will never be bored! Superstars are full of ideas and electricity. They can dispense with you, however, if you are not useful and cannot keep up. Working for a Superstar is an endless challenge that will always engage you. It helps to learn as much as you can, for Superstars have a great deal to prove and challenge you on. If clever and subtle, you can learn a great deal from them, and your experience can look good on a résumé. Be a resource, but don't expect a great deal of acknowledgment or recognition.

If you work with *a Superstar* . . . be prepared for perpetual competition! Superstars have to be first. Collaborate with a Superstar, and you may create a synergy that will result in both prestige and money for your company. Superstars are exploiters who view you as an extension of their needs, so if you don't need to be first, and don't have to take all the credit and recognition, working with them can be a humbling but stimulating road to growth—that is, if you *can* work with them.

If you supervise *a Superstar* . . . be careful—he or she may be after your job! Do not underestimate Superstars' ambition, but give them a chance to shine and grow, because you—and the company—could be the beneficiary. Just don't expect long-term loyalty. As long as they are rewarded either financially or by challenges for growth, Superstars will try their best. Take them out to lunch, ask questions, find out what their dreams and hopes are, and see if it is practical to help them realize their goals.

The Precisionist

Precisionists are principled, idealistic, and conscientious, with a strong sense of right and wrong. Frequently advocates and agents for change, they are always striving to improve things but afraid of making a mistake. Moral and ethical, critical and meticulous, Precisionists are well organized, orderly, and fastidious but can also be impersonal, rigid, and emotionally constricted. They are true perfectionists in every way. With strong opinions about the world and a subjective, yet unyielding opinion of what's right and what's wrong, they can be prone to anger and impatience.

Here are the traits to look for in the writing of a Precisionist:

- Deliberately formed letters
- Well-organized space patterns
- Precise writing
- Legible text
- Attention to punctuation and i-dots and t-bars
- Good spatial judgment
- Arcade and/or garland connection

Examples of Precisionists are Martha Stewart, Thomas Edison, Linda Wachner, and Rudy Giuliani.

A Portrait of a Precisionist:
THOMAS EDISON

This scientist and inventor is known for creating the incandescent lamp, the phonograph, and the development of talking films. Thomas Edison's precision is seen by his rigid letters, which are small and carefully written. Each detail is attended to: every *T* is crossed, each *i* is dotted. There is great legibility to the writing as it is important that his message be properly conveyed. The writing is also well organized on the page.

The long and strong t-bars show his determination. In his signature, the thickening t-bar in *Thomas* reveals his need to impose himself on this environment, permitting nothing to deter him from his endeavors. The slant is upright, the script is uniform, and the strong pressure indicates Edison's energy, perseverance, resoluteness, and dominance. The baseline is steady and the movement slow and careful, so you can see that he is a thinking type who, while deliberate in approach, can process information easily. The uniformity of the letters in his text and signature suggests a lack of spontaneity, which is an inherent quality of a precisionist.

The space between the lines reveals Edison's capacity to detach if necessary. This is a necessary and beneficial trait to a scientist, because it brings objectivity to any pursuit.

Getting Along with a Precisionist

If you work for *a Precisionist* . . . be organized, keep lists, find ways of reporting and measuring your outcomes. Understand that Precisionists often suffer from anxiety, and the need for perfection is a need for control and often approval.

If you work with *a Precisionist* . . . be prepared to be frustrated by what you see as unnecessarily high, unrealistic standards—they're Precisionists, remember? Do your best to ride with it. Know that Precisionists have an insatiable need to continue to prove themselves, so you must develop detachment and suspend your judgment.

If you supervise *a Precisionist* . . . be nurturing, reassuring, and appreciative. Be patient, because Precisionists will not change and can be very trying. Discuss your expectations and the best use of their time. Make it clear as to what you believe is counterproductive in their approach. Be quick to insist that they join a gym or visit a spa, because they need a routine of release for tension.

The Team Player

Team Players are essential to any work environment. They equate their personal goals with their company's long-term objectives and success. They believe they will benefit most if the company prospers. Without the safety of the company around them, they can often feel insignificant and lost. They worry about corporate projects, interpersonal relationships, and their own careers. Though they are motivated by the prospect of success, they frequently lack risk-taking abilities, toughness, detachment, confidence, and the energy required to reach the top.

Here are the traits to look for in the writing of a Team Player:

- Garland and/or thread connection
- Legibility
- Good pressure
- Movement to the right
- Tendency toward school type letters

Examples of Team players include Magic Johnson, Richard Gephardt, and Ted Williams.

A Portrait of a Team Player:
TED WILLIAMS

I've found in life the more you practice the better you get, if you want something enough + work hard to get it your chances of success are much greater.

Ted Williams

Baseball legend Ted Williams's writing connection is school type, showing his conventionality. The signature is very consistent with the text, showing that "what you see is what you get." There is no great inconsistency between Williams's self-image and the way he publicly presents himself.

It is interesting that the connection of letters is so strong there is no break between the first and last name of his signature. Look at the high i-dots, showing high standards. The letter connections show his focus and determination, and the slant to the right indicates his need for approval. The baseline is uneven, revealing a variety of moods.

We know that Williams was a team player because we don't see signs of a strong ego in the writing, which means that, although he was an outstanding team star, he was content to blend in with the others. He didn't want to make waves, as seen by the relative conventionality of the writing. Although there is no question that he was an athlete of great ability, the writing pattern shows his need to collaborate with his teammates. The space between the lines indicates awareness of others.

Getting Along with a Team Player

If you work for *a Team Player* . . . be of help whenever possible. Team Players can easily see you as someone who can make them look good. Try not to take advantage of them, which is easy to do because they are so anxious to please. Make them feel included and important, and they will reward you.

If you work with *a Team Player* . . . you shouldn't have too difficult a time. Include Team Players, reassure them, publicly recognize them—they are motivated by approval and a need to belong.

If you supervise *a Team Player* . . . understand that Team Players don't mind taking orders. They don't often want to lead or make unpopular decisions. So you can relax in the knowledge that they are not after your job. Be sure to give them the resources necessary to do their work—they are there to help make you look good!

The Trailblazer

The typical Trailblazer is playful, industrious, fair, enthusiastic, and open to new concepts. Trailblazers have an independent streak and are highly creative, with ideas that are often on the cutting edge. They march to the beat of their own internal drummer and are oblivious to time, deadlines, or the needs of others. While they can be charismatic and fun, they work better alone and can be self-absorbed. They are bored by the mundane and predictable, and have an adolescent aversion to authority.

Here are the traits to look for in the writing of a Trailblazer:

- Highly original letter connections and letter formations
- Often upright slant
- Writing can be illegible
- Unconventional use of space
- Strong pressure

Examples of Trailblazers include Steven Spielberg, Walt Disney, Norman Lear, and Andy Warhol.

A Portrait of a Trailblazer:
WALT DISNEY

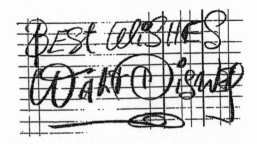

Animation king Walt Disney displays middle-zone writing, which is often a sign of self-centeredness. His need for space is seen in the way the writing takes over the page. The paraph under his signature further underscores a need for attention.

Playfulness is shown in the charming rhythm, as well as the creative letterforms. The *W* in *Walt* and the *D* in *Disney* are like musical notes. The whole writing looks like it has been painted with a paintbrush. There is liveliness and great energy to the writing pattern.

Disney's independence is confirmed by the baseline. Although the sample was written on lined paper, the lines are ignored, showing that he went his own way and did not want to be bound or dictated to.

The writing is idiosyncratic, as revealed by the unusual line in the letter *B* in *Best* and the circular i-dots. The large *s*'s in the word *wishes* show that no one told Disney what to do. The *s* or last letter becomes larger, as another way of imposing himself on the page. Each of the three *e*'s on the page is different, indicating as well his creativity, multifaceted personality, and changeability.

Getting Along with a Trailblazer

If you work for *a Trailblazer* . . . Remember that Trailblazers require structure, privacy, security, patience, and contracts. Trailblazers are often disorganized and volatile, with chaotic work habits. Their extreme absorption in their own ideas or vision can cause them to be oblivious to the needs of others. With a Trailblazer you will never be bored, but you must also be prepared to be flexible, patient, and understanding. If Trailblazers respect and value you, you could be in for a rocket ride that will compensate you for the frustrations.

View Trailblazers as laws unto themselves and withhold judgment. They are fascinating spirits—Peter Pans with streaks of genius. Be of help and support, and you will always have interesting stories to tell.

If you work with *a Trailblazer* . . . recognize that Trailblazers are difficult to work with because they are often loners; be prepared to be a resource to them. Like Superstars, Trailblazers tend to see you as an extension of their needs. Your days with them are likely to be nonroutine because their sense of time is skewed. They are often more interested in work and achievements than in having a personal life and assume you feel the same way.

Trailblazers are often lonely and alienated, so give them your support if you believe in them—you may be part of an extraordinary discovery.

If you supervise *a Trailblazer* . . . give them structure, space, opportunities to fail without reprimand or judgment, financial security, and patience to ride out the storms. Because Trailblazers are groundbreaking thinkers, you might also want to secure legal contracts for your ideas and discoveries, so that you can reap the rewards of your investment in them.

Trailblazers dislike authority and cannot be reined in. Find out their dreams, and if you believe in them, think of Trailblazers as undervalued stock that may reward you many times over in time.

The Prober

Probers are alert, insightful, curious, and able to concentrate well and master complex concepts. They thrive on facts, figures, research, and analysis. Because they have innovative and inventive minds, Probers are frequently preoccupied with their own thoughts and objectives. They think with their heads rather than their hearts, which makes them rational and intellectual but not in touch with their own emotions or those of others.

Here are the traits to look for in the writing of a Prober:

- Upright slant
- Often introvert typology
- Wide space between words
- Clear, well-organized space picture
- Often small, narrow letter formations

Examples of Probers include Albert Einstein, Benjamin Cardozo, Sir Edmund Hillary, and James Watson.

A Portrait of a Prober:
ALBERT EINSTEIN

First and foremost, Albert Einstein was alert—his writing contains sharp, original forms and connections, which are particularly notable in the signature.

His concentration was keen, seen by the small, precise letters and the overconnection of letters. Einstein was independent, which we see in the upright slant. This is also shown in the space between words. His innovative skills are seen in the signature, which is highly original. The *t* in *Einstein* has the t-bar off the stem, indicating aspiration, enthusiasm, and imagination. Clarity of thought is shown in the fine space between the words and lines. The small, meticulous, precise letters show exacting standards— every *i* is dotted and every *t* is crossed, showing respect for detail.

The space between Einstein's words demonstrates the ability and pride in being an iconoclast. The small letters also show independence of thought and no great need for approval or definition by others. This can be equated with a preoccupation with thought, or living in the world of the mind, the most comfortable home for the Prober.

Getting Along with a Prober

If you work for *a Prober* . . . find out what they want and ask what he or she needs. Explain the rewards and positive consequences of achieving what you want. Remember to leave Probers alone and give them plenty of space. Be prepared to do tons of research and to work long hours, with the possibility of working on their timetable. Realize you are in the company of an extraordinary mind; no doubt, the experience will stretch your mind, help you grow, and look impressive on your résumé.

If you work with *a Prober* . . . it can be stimulating and exciting. Probers are unconventional and restless, and have insatiable curiosity. When working with a Prober, you will be constantly challenged. Like Trailblazers, they keep their own timetables. If you are willing to put aside personal needs to collaborate with them on research, fact finding, and implementation of their ideas, you could be well rewarded.

If you supervise *a Prober* . . . think of him or her as a troubleshooter. Offer challenges and freedom, and the necessary tools. Probers can be invaluable in solving problems that would stump less agile minds. Take advantage of their creativity and uniqueness, suspend judgment and protocol—they are laws unto themselves!

The Peacemaker

The Peacemaker is the opposite of the Mover and Shaker. People turn to Peacemakers because they deal with things in a calm, easygoing, accommodating manner. Accepting, trusting, good-natured, and supportive, they can be too willing to go along to keep the peace. Peacemakers strive to simplify problems and minimize discord. They are adept at problem solving and resolution. Creatures of habit, they can be passive, stubborn, and unwilling to change, and at their worst, inattentive and neglectful. Peacemakers perform best when they are able to resolve conflicts and bring people together.

Here are the traits to look for in the writing of a Peacemaker:

- Pure garland or angle and garland connections
- Careful, deliberate writing
- No entangling lines between sentences
- Refined letter patterns
- Well-organized writing
- Good spatial picture

Examples of Peacemakers include Bill Clinton, Jimmy Carter, and George Lucas.

A Portrait of a Peacemaker:
JIMMY CARTER

The extreme right slant of former President Jimmy Carter's handwriting shows his need to reach out to others and gain their approval.

The connection is garland and sometimes thread, which we know represents one who hates conflict and needs harmony. The height of the upper zone reveals his idealism. The careful design of each letter indicates a need to do well, and the space picture reveals emotional clarity. The constriction of the letters can indicate stubbornness, and their overconnection can show indomitability. The height of the cross over the *J* in his signature shows that Carter's reach can often exceed his grasp.

Getting Along with a Peacemaker

If you work for *a Peacemaker* . . . do not show your irritation with his or her word games, strategies, and verbal volleying. Get to know the Peacemaker's style of communication and the psychology behind it, so if it catches you off guard or annoys you, you won't let your true feelings slip. If you become emotionally transparent, they will react negatively and you'll wind up paying the price.

If you work with *a Peacemaker* . . . ask what role she or he expects you to assume and always be there as a backup. Do your homework, think of it as a role to play, and be there so you can be trusted as a support.

If you supervise *a Peacemaker* . . . be aware that timing will be the biggest challenge—make sure she or he understands your timetable and parameters. Peacemakers may waffle more than other types. Try not to lose patience with their need to see all sides of an issue before arriving at an outcome.

The Art of Negotiation

Chances are that at some point you're going to have to be involved in a negotiation. Whether you're looking for a raise or a promotion, closing a deal with a client or vendor, trying to land a new job, or even attempting to get a better buy on office equipment, negotiating skills are valuable. You can use these skills when you're buying a house, browsing at a garage sale, or even looking to make a date with someone!

Even if you're confident about your negotiating skills, you can gain the upper hand by getting a little inside information about the hidden needs of the person with whom you're going to be negotiating. Graphology can give you that edge.

As we know, negotiations are seldom swift and simple. So, whatever the circumstances, the more information you have about "the other party," the likelier your chances are to leverage a better deal or outcome.

Now that you've learned more about the eight business personalities—and have been able to recognize which personality best reflects whoever holds a position that influences your job—here are some tips on how you can use your newfound knowledge as leverage when the time is right (and we all know, timing is everything!). Certain negotiating strategies will work for two or more personality types. And keep in mind that some types shy away from having to negotiate altogether.

Negotiating with a Mover and Shaker or a Superstar

Movers and Shakers and Superstars are pragmatic and strongly interested in the bottom line. They want to learn and have extraordinary focus. And, unlike most people, they are usually energized by stress. They always have more than one plan, and any problem they encounter is a solution in disguise. They are conscious of and make maximum use of their time.

In a negotiation, the Movers and Shakers' or Superstars' objective is to win at all costs. While you might think that this would make any negotiation a fruitless pursuit, think again. To these personalities, negotiating is a game to be won or lost, and they need a way to keep score. That score is determined by one key point or issue. If you can identify that issue and are willing to acquiesce on that point, they will become flexible on other matters. While they want to win, they also believe they can change your way of thinking. So by letting them triumph over that key point, you've shown that you've come around to their viewpoint.

Another useful tip—don't indulge in small talk. You are there to negotiate, not chat. Don't overload these personalities with data either. Movers and Shakers and Superstars don't need to be weighted down with minutiae—they tend to make quick decisions on the basic facts.

Negotiating with a Firecracker

It's not easy to negotiate with Firecrackers. They tend to conceal their real motives, so you have to have alternate plans ready. Besides, they are notorious for changing their minds, so be prepared for anything.

Firecrackers need to be acknowledged in a negotiation. They don't like to be taken advantage of and get irritated if you try to beat them at their own game or even try to play the game the way they do. Your best strategy is to convince them with data that your plan, idea, or recommendation is going to support their long-range objectives, and consequently save time and money (or result in payback or a profit). Provide them with all the benefits up front and in the most enthusiastic way possible. If they like you and see merit in your ideas, they might give you some of what you want.

Negotiating with a Precisionist or a Prober

Precisionists and Probers don't care for the push and pull of a negotiation. Orderly and detailed-oriented, they prefer that everything be perfectly in place and not disrupted. They have their own modus operandi and arrive at conclusions in their own way, in their own time, unconscious of the needs or desires of others. Their attention to detail and data gives them leeway to change their minds when confronted with new information. So just when you think you've come to a decision or compromise, watch out—it's apt to change.

When negotiating with these personalities, do your homework and check for accuracy. Precisionists and Probers thrive on details, so provide facts and figures, and back up your position with as many solid details as possible—they will need to see all the data and weigh every option. By understanding how they operate and playing to their needs and criteria, you can greatly facilitate the negotiation. Precisionists and Probers are tough but not immovable. Good luck!

Negotiating with a Team Player or a Peacemaker

Team Players and Peacemakers usually want what's fair and equitable to everyone. They like win-win scenarios. If you find yourself having to negotiate with them, be sure to point out how what you are asking for or offering benefits not only them but also everyone with whom they come in contact—they often care more about relationships than about results. Personal chemistry is very important to Team Players and Peacemakers—you must appeal to their emotions while challenging their intellects. And don't mistake friendliness for weakness—it's not, and if you lose sight of that, you'll put yourself at a disadvantage.

Proceed slowly and wait until you sense their trust. Demonstrate that you really care about people. Don't pressure Team Players and Peacemakers, because they usually need time to think things through. They are on their own timetable, so you might have to wait until they are comfortable with you or with what you are proposing.

Negotiating with a Trailblazer

Trailblazers can be difficult to negotiate with. They are so focused on their own thoughts and ideas that they are not adept at dealing with people, much less negotiating with them. If you have to negotiate with Trailblazers, let them take the lead as to the time and place, even if it's after hours. Show them, in concrete ways, how your ideas or requests will be of benefit to them and their objectives.

The Signs of Success

You're probably wondering; Is there a way graphology can help me to determine my own level of success? Yes! Throughout this book you've learned about writing patterns and characteristics and what they tell you about a writer's personality. If you examine your own writing, you're apt to find strengths, assets, weaknesses, and liabilities. Examining and uncovering these traits could help you to hone your best qualities and skills; break free from old, restrictive patterns; and avoid mistakes. Don't, however, rush to judgment; it's always best to consult a graphology book or a professional. Developing your skill in handwriting analysis takes a lot of practice, but when mastered, it will reward you many times over!

PEN POINT   Handwriting and the Entrepreneur

About a decade ago the graphologists Felix Klein, Roger Rubin, and I designed a research study involving handwriting and the entrepreneur, which was published in *The Journal of Perceptual and Motor Skills*. The study concluded that there were, indeed, a variety of handwriting indicators that most entrepreneurs share. They include exaggeration of capital letters, strong pressure on the page, a sharp right slant, and a more idiosyncratic style.

Handwriting traits that revealed a fear of failure were equally prevalent. Among them: narrow margins, letters, words, and spacing; slow speed, small capital letters, left trend, letters that slant in different directions, compressed writing pattern, and retraced letters.

The following traits typically appear in the handwriting of people who are risk taking, resourceful, tenacious, outgoing, and with other qualities that lead to success in business, and in life. Do they show up in the writing of your friends or co-workers? Do some of these traits show up in your own writing?

Risk Taker

- Original forms
- Moderate to strong pressure
- Tall upper zone
- Good rhythm with rightward movement

Independent

- Simplified forms
- Strong initial letters
- Strong final strokes

Resourceful

- Balance between zones
- Strong capital letters
- Simplified letterforms
- Garland or primary thread connection

Confident with Strong Self-Esteem

- Good rhythm and form
- Consistent pressure
- Fluid movement
- Large capital letters
- Signature larger than rest of writing

Tenacious

- Consistent form and pressure
- Steady baseline and rhythm
- Strong final strokes
- T-bars with hooks
- Overconnected letterforms

Self-Motivating

- Moderate to heavy pressure
- Original and creative forms
- Fast writing
- Good arrangement of words on the page

Outgoing

- Rightward movement
- Larger than average writing size
- Need for lots of space on the page

Energetic and Ready for Action

- Fast speed
- Original but simplified forms
- Right slant

Forward Thinking

- Tall upper zone
- Strong rhythm
- Arcade connection
- Right trend

Chances are you'll see some signs of success in your own writing. Then you'll be inspired by these positive traits and work toward strengthening any weak areas you have.

With the state of the economy continually fluctuating and companies coming and going, it's always beneficial to recognize your skills, abilities, and personal strengths so that you can have the confidence to find—or even create—opportunities for yourself. The world needs entrepreneurs now more than ever. Perhaps you can be one of them!

Whom Should You Hire?

Let's assume you are an entrepreneur and need to hire a second-in-command to help you increase your business, make it more efficient, or help manage your business. Who's the best person for the job?

Here's an exercise that will help you make better decisions about the people whom you employ. Following are two sets of handwriting samples from prospective employees. Examine each set and select the handwriting that you feel belongs to the best candidate.

Applicant Set A

A1

> To achieve excellence, you must stick to your own TRUE North - your own core principles and values. If you do - - it will guide you as you make decisions on the margin. It will give you the courage to always find the truth, look it square in the eye and stick to it even when it's hard. If you use and project the power that comes with confidence then no matter what you face, you will be unique and remarkable

A2

> plan from five years ago, and an anniversary card my husband sent me last year. I have nothing written by my mother or father in the house.

Did you choose A1 or A2?

If you picked A1 . . . this sample belongs to Orit Gadiesh, the CEO of the consulting firm Bain & Company.

There is a lot of angularity in the lower zone, signifying assertion. Gadiesh knows how to make things happen. He is very smart, and his interesting writing connections are highly simplified.

Look at how self-contained and contracted the writing sample is. Gadiesh is aloof and keeps his distance from people. Everything is small and upright, compressed inside that square on the page, which means he lives very much inside himself.

Gadiesh is extremely intelligent, as seen in the sophistication, creativity, and simplification of the letterforms. The margins represent his protection against the impositions of others. This is not a glad-hander or backslapper. Gadiesh is very efficient and direct, handling what is necessary—and handling it well—thereby conserving his energy. He knows how to delegate and analyze things effectively.

In the words "Find the truth" (the sixth line from the bottom), there is a high degree of simplicity. The wide spaces between words and narrow letters show his distance from others.

If you picked A2 . . . this is the handwriting of an anonymous fifty-year-old man, although there are many women who have his writing style. The writing is conventional and its speed is slow, showing perfectionism. The beginning strokes and carefully drawn letters indicate that this is someone who is risk-adverse. The right slant shows a need for approval and an unwillingness to tolerate the loneliness of leadership and the consequences of making an unpopular decision.

Conclusion

Even though he works better alone, Applicant A1 would be a better hire than A2. A1 brings intelligence, analytical and managerial skills, and knows how to delegate. Applicant A2 is far more timid in his approach to management and leadership nor likely to be a creative or driving force in your business.

Applicant Set B

B1 *TO Arlyn*
Best Wishes

B2 *Dear Arlyn,*
I hope to go to Italy! My family loves me. I am on "Good Day New York" every morning. I am happy that you start your day with me! Tune in everyday at 5:30 am and we will give you all the latest information and breaking news.

Did you choose B1 or B2?

If you picked B1 . . . This sample is by the former "First Daughter" of Ronald Reagan, Patti Davis. People with this writing style are self-indulgent and narcissistic. Davis is a feeling typology who needs a lot of attention and recognition. Her immaturity is revealed by the large middle zone and by the need to impose herself on the page. The space picture is poor, showing little room for emotional clarity or awareness of others. There is almost no upper zone, which indicates disregard for authority and rules, and confused values.

This writing shows lack of development, simplification, and style. The rhythm is labored, which means she would accomplish her tasks slowly. The round, full letters indicate oral writing, which reveals that her early needs for communication were not met, and consequently, she can be high-maintenance.

If you picked B2 . . . this sample is the writing of Lyn Brown, a television anchor on *Good Day New York*. This is an active, energetic, feminine writing of a woman who knows what she wants and knows how to get it. There is grace and good rhythm in the writing. One reason Brown would be a good employee is that she is dynamic and won't take no for an answer, as seen in the highly connected letters and movement to the right, toward one's goals and the future. The connectedness shows her persistence.

This writer is unstoppable! She processes information quickly. Note the speed yet legibility of the writing; she makes no mistakes. Her pride is shown in the size of the initial letters, especially the *A* in *Arlyn*. This size reveals her high standards. Do not cross her, however, by promising her something and not giving it to her. The overconnection of the letters shows that her word is her bond. She will keep it with you, and she expects you to keep your promises as well.

Conclusion

If you needed a reliable, hardworking, and disciplined individual, you would likely hire Lyn Brown. Patti Davis's personality would be more suited to working for herself or running her own business, which might well be done with style and flair.

CHAPTER 7

You Can Choose Your Friends . . .

You can choose your friends, but you can't choose your family! Who cares for you unselfishly, and who is purely self-serving? What makes your spouse tick? How can you get along better with your mother-in-law or any in-law? Is there an easier way to understand your brooding teen or appease your aging parents' anxieties? Family dynamics critically affect our lives. Understanding what motivates significant others, what they need and expect, and how to improve communications with them can greatly enhance our happiness and peace of mind. This chapter helps you learn more about the pivotal people in your life by examining their handwritings. Samples will reveal personality traits and interpersonal dynamics.

Happiness is having a large, loving, caring, close-knit family . . . in another city.

—GEORGE BURNS

TODAY FAMILY DYNAMICS are more complex than ever. Only a few generations ago, the nuclear family consisted of a mother, father, and children, with two sets of grandparents, an aunt or uncle, and a handful of cousins. However, with the rise in divorce rates (50 percent of all marriages) and with remarriages a common occurrence, there are now more "blended" families, consisting of parents, stepparents, half or stepsiblings, and in-laws. Moreover, since we now live longer, chances are that even great-grandparents factor into the equation. The more people in your immediate family, the more issues and challenges are likely to arise. Spousal and parent-child relationships are already complex, so the addition of new and extended family members to the fold can often lead to conflicts, miscommunications, jealousies, and a lot of hurt feelings all around.

Even if you think you know your family well, there's always something that may surprise you. Perhaps you come from a family where people don't express what they think or feel, or one in which there are lots of big secrets and problems get swept under the rug. Or else you come from a household of screamers—outbursts blow over but never lead to calm discussions. Were your parents overprotective, or were they so involved with their own lives that you felt neglected or irrelevant? Do you have a sister or brother who always has to one-up you? Or a younger sibling who gets away with things you would be punished for? Are you suspicious that your spouse is having an affair or hiding something from you? Does your teenager have problems he or she is keeping from you?

If these or other family issues affect you, it's time to try a bit of graphological insight. Using graphology to learn more about individuals is very effective, but it can also help you to see the larger pattern of family dynamics. Not everything is equal in a family. No one truly gets along the same with everyone in a household or extended family. You're always apt to have conflicts with or preferences toward someone, even if outwardly you seem to do a good job of being impartial or keeping the peace.

Family Dynamics in Action: The Kennedys

In order to see the underlying conditions that quietly affect family relationships, let's examine the Kennedys. This famous family is a good example of how parents, children, and in-laws relate (or, as the case may be, do not). The Kennedys epitomized both the best of America and its reckless worst. Were the Kennedys cursed, or as many have said, did their insatiable desire for power put them at risk?

JOSEPH KENNEDY:
Dynamic Patriarch

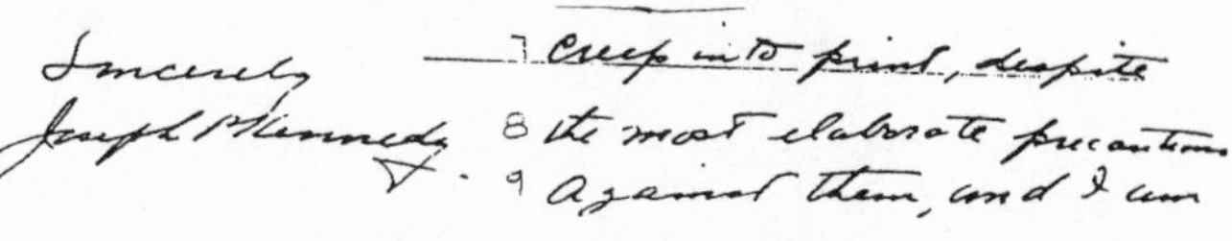

[handwritten signature: Sincerely, Joseph Kennedy] *[handwritten note:] creep into print, despite 8 the most elaborate precautions 9 against them, and I am*

Patriarch Joseph Kennedy raised his offspring to believe they were invulnerable and could make their own rules. His dynasty was rich, powerful, beautiful, and doomed.

Joe's writing is dynamic, strong, aggressive, and entrepreneurial. He was an intuitive type, and his writing's movement to the right shows that he was determined to achieve his objectives and overcome challenges. The writing also reveals creativity and an ability to develop original ideas.

When Joe was a student at Harvard, he was blackballed from one of the college's elite social clubs because he was Irish Catholic—a snub that he would spend the rest of his life avenging. Look at the harpoon (long, hooked, strokes below the baseline) in the lower zone of his signature—it is a spear with which to capture his prey! The small letters and speed reflect his determination, focus, and desire to win at all costs. Although capable of aggression and ruthlessness, his writing also shows he could be smooth and charming as evidenced by the easy rhythm and connections.

The organization and clarity of the writing are also impressive. You can sense the speed to reach his goals. T-bars are sometimes connected to the first letters of the following words, showing his enthusiasm and ability to communicate. Dynamic and energetic, Joseph Kennedy craved activity. His keen intellect and ability to articulate issues and take risks contributed to his great financial success. His love of money is confirmed by the size of the *J* in the lower zone of his signature.

ROSE KENNEDY:
The Hand That Rocked the Cradle

Rose Kennedy was very rigid, tough, and compulsive. A thinking type, she was extraordinarily focused on what mattered to her at whether to stay at the Ritz or at Claridges. I like a quiet hotel and I love to walk every day — I vaguely remember the Ritz is near the Park. As soon as I decide, I shall communicate with you

In my renewed thanks to you, my dear May — I want to take this occasion to tell you how very much your friendship means to Joe — He will never forget the letter you wrote to him last year when Jack lay desperately ill —

Sincerely,
Rose

of welcoming you at our house some time soon. Again my thanks and my best remembrances.
Very sincerely,
Rose Kennedy

the moment. Rose realized her agenda by unyielding obsessiveness, as revealed by the overconnection and pressure of her strokes on the page. She was without the slightest bit of compassion. She wanted what she wanted when she wanted it.

This was not a woman known for nurturing, patience, or sensitivity to the needs of others. She had high expectations and high standards. She maintained strict rules and regulations, which helped her survive the many crises she endured during her lifetime.

When asked by noted historian Doris Kearns Goodwin what was the greatest disappointment of her life, Rose did not say the early deaths of four of her children or the institutionalization of her daughter Rosemary but the prevention of her going to Wellesley College. Her father, John Francis "Honey Fitz" Fitzgerald, the mayor of Boston, was told that it was only proper for his Catholic daughter to attend Sacred Heart Academy, a school that stressed faith, discipline, and religious standards. Rose believed Wellesley would open and expand her mind, whereas Sacred Heart closed it. Her handwriting shows a woman who was neither emotionally released nor in touch with her feelings.

Sacred Heart no doubt gave her the fortitude to deal with her husband's peccadilloes and dark side. Jacqueline Kennedy recalled Rose once saying, "I will never let anyone feel sorry for me!"

Joseph met his match in Rose! Theirs was a marriage of commitment but without much emotional content or intimacy. Gloria Swanson, one of Joe's most notable mistresses, who actually accompanied the couple on a cruise, was quoted as saying, "Either Rose Kennedy is a complete fool or a better actress than I will ever be!" No doubt Rose had discipline and an iron will. Her stoicism is confirmed in the upright slant of her writing, which also reflects her self-discipline.

Hers is the artificial, controlled writing of a woman who suffered in silence. In the lower zone, you see the angle, the harpoon, and the fishhook, reflective of her hidden anger, tenacity, and resilience.

*   *   *

DID YOU KNOW?

Planes have been an ominous metaphor for death and loss in the Kennedy family. Joe Kennedy Jr. died when his plane exploded on a secret mission during World War II. Kathleen Kennedy, the brightest and most spirited of the Kennedy women, met her death flying with her lover to the south of France for a holiday. Ted Kennedy had a plane accident that resulted in severe injuries to his back and many hospitalizations. And, of course, there was the tragic death of John Kennedy Jr. when he lost control of the plane he was flying just miles from Hyannisport in 1999.

*   *   *

JOHN F. KENNEDY:
The Prodigal Son

John Kennedy was very much influenced by his father—even in his writing! If you compare the two samples, you'll observe his has some of the same speed, threads, and brilliance as seen in his father's writing. He loved ideas and relished approaching a problem or challenge, seeing it as a mind game. Joseph Sr. was street smart, whereas John was much more cerebral, with more of an ability to adjust to situations and people. Joseph Kennedy did not have that flexibility; once he made up his mind, it was hard for him to change it.

The dynamic between Joe and John was of the son modeling himself unconsciously after his father. We see from their writing that they were both charming but cold, brilliant but not introspective. There is much movement in the writing with a thrust toward the right, which shows a need to reach outer goals and objectives. Their energies and drives were focused on the future.

Joe instilled in his sons his ideas of machismo. Women were objects, goals were to be reached with a disregard for anyone who got in their way. The speed and neglect in John Kennedy's writing show a personal recklessness and disregard for consequences.

ROBERT AND ETHEL KENNEDY:
The Woman Behind the Man

Robert Kennedy

Going back to 10/28/77
~~and only terrible noise~~. . . . .

When I look at all the prisoners in kings County Hospital. I cannot help but feel sorry for them. Their like lost souls; many in and out. of institutions for all of their lives; little hope, no family, no friends.

I think people only want peace and comfort in life but apparently few know how to find it. It seems like the only saviour these patients have is thorazine but they really need Jesus.

I never thought my life would turn out like ~~this~~ - what a mess.

If it wasn't for my family and their love, and

Ethel Kennedy

What was the dynamic behind the relationship of Robert Kennedy and his wife, Ethel? Ethel's writing is somewhat reminiscent of Rose Kennedy's—controlled, rigid, upright, deliberate, and compressed. So, in a sense, Bobby married the image of his mother! Though it doesn't have the same underlying anger seen in Rose's script, Ethel's writing similarly suggests a strict Catholic upbringing.

Bobby's writing is dynamic and inhibited. He had the narrow writing of an introvert. Ethel, basically a sensate typology, is very extroverted, and also competitive and intense. Her writing is carefully designed, written slowly and with much thought. Bobby's writing is fast, dynamic, and contracted. Despite these differences, their samples reveal that they were both tense and intense.

As we know, Bobby's relationship with his brother John was one of high regard. Bobby admired John's style and his smoothness in personal interactions. But while John's simple, easygoing intellectual skills, irony, and subtle humor came effortlessly, Bobby had to work hard; everything he achieved was done with single-mindedness, energy, and drive. Bobby could be vicious and aggressive, as seen in his narrow and angular letters and writing pressure. He could also hold a grudge, which is shown in the tight control of the letters. His small letters reveal him to be a thinking type. Bobby was serious, always ruminating and analyzing, while John was stylish and fun loving.

Bobby was also intense. He believed in things with utter conviction. His stilted writing reflects his inflexibility, and rigid people tend to be extremely committed.

Devoted to her husband, Ethel fueled Bobby's competitive spirit, giving him unconditional love, and becoming even more politically ambitious for him than he was for himself. Her ambitions for him were ways to channel her own energies away from his infidelities and toward her goal: the White House.

Ethel's natural competitiveness was reflected in her relationship with her mother-in-law. It was said that Ethel had eleven children because she wanted to outdo the nine Rose produced!

As we will shortly see, unlike her sister-in-law Jacqueline, Ethel was completely wrapped up in her husband's life, which no doubt helped him develop out of the shadows of his superstar brothers Joe Jr. and John and into the limelight.

EDWARD AND JOAN KENNEDY:
Mismatched Marriage

Ted Kennedy was reputed to have had second thoughts about marrying Joan, but her father pressured him to see it through. Ted

despise war for war denies the
vividness of life. And he had
a special affection for children
for they held the promise of life.

We all realize that many
other considerations fall within
your responsibility and that of the
Court. But if the kind of man
my brother was is pertinent we
believe it should be weighted in
the balance on the side of.
compassion, mercy and God's gift
of life itself.

Sincerely,

Edward M. Kennedy

best wishes from

Joan Kennedy

Kennedy's early writing does not have a particular intellectual
bent. Unlike that of his father and brothers, his writing does not
evidence much character or precision. It is school type writing.

There is nothing creative about it; the unnecessary lead-in strokes in the letters *t* and *i* reflect Ted Kennedy as a man in his thirties with immaturity and insecurity.

However, the sample on the next page represents more development and angularity, which reveal that Ted had come a long way. It also illustrates the importance of having writing samples from various stages in a person's life. The early sample of Ted's writing is soft, weak, and indifferent.

In Joan Kennedy's writing, there are a lot of separations in the words. The capitals in her signature drift. Hers is a feeling typology. The writing looks delicate and does not reflect resilience. Stress is her enemy, and it has been excessive in her life: she had a child with cancer, an unfaithful husband, the scandal of Chappaquiddick, and the pressure of an imposing, often judgmental family. Unlike the vitality in her mother-in-law's writing, Joan's writing pressure is weak and lacking a strong sense of structure. For short periods of time she could buoy herself up, but her resilience was hard to sustain. It is no secret that she had drinking problems. Joan's writing is not well integrated; it is an upright print script, showing she was trying to hold herself together. She and Ted eventually divorced.

Joseph Kennedy's patriarchal fantasies and ambitions were, to a great extent, lived out by his three eldest sons, Joe Jr. (the patriarch's original choice for president, until his aircraft was shot down), John, and Bobby. Ted remained "the baby"; less was expected of him. Then, after his brothers' deaths, he became the last great hope of the Kennedy dynasty. But Ted had been so protected and indulged, and had to live in the shadows of his famous and publicly revered brothers, that he responded with rebelliousness and foolish, adolescent behavior. However, despite his mishaps, missteps, and responsibilities as the father figure to twenty-seven children (the children of his siblings, living and deceased, as well as his own), Ted emerged as a survivor. And in terms of political power, as a senator with great seniority, he became a credit to his state and to the family name.

Ted's writing becomes more angular, and much more defined, with a stronger definition in the upper zone and a definite roundness in that zone reflecting creative fantasy. He changed from being an errant, naughty boy to someone more responsible and focused. His later sample is a sharper, more evolved signature, revealing a higher level of ambition, resiliency, vision, and aspiration. It has a lot more structure. His original typology was of an intuitive, but he evolved into a thinking type—if you carefully compare both samples, you'll see this evolution.

In the early writing his dislike of responsibility is seen in the softness of the strokes—the writing has no central core. It is thready and ambiguous, and the letters seem to drift aimlessly. In the second sample, there is more angularity and narrowness of letters. The space between the letters gets smaller, while the height of the letters, especially the upper-zone letters, gets larger.

In both signatures—"Edward Kennedy" and "Ted Kennedy"—note the initial letters, which are very big. They show pride in his accomplishments.

JACQUELINE KENNEDY:
First Lady of Camelot

Jacqueline Kennedy, a woman who grew up with a dashing, dark father (nicknamed "Black Jack" Bouvier) realized early on the unpredictability and infidelity in her parents' marriage. Although they divorced, her father remained a great love in her life. When she married another Jack (John Kennedy's nickname), she knew

June 18

Dear Stanley

At last - the book I longed for more than any other!

I plan to conspicuously leave it on the coffee table to impress all.

I did enjoy so much sitting next to you and I do think the evening made Ros very happy.

With so many thanks

Jackie

all too well that men like her husband and father do not change, so she negotiated a livable arrangement.

Jackie, like her mother-in-law, adapted to her husband's freewheeling ways by seeking freedom and solace through trips abroad, shopping sprees, and escapes from boring White House duties (which her sister-in-law Ethel had so deeply craved). Her generous allowances from her husband and father-in-law helped her to weather personal humiliations, rumors, and scandals.

As noted in Chapter 3, Jackie's writing is sensate and very connected although with nice breaks. There is a fine sense of space, which indicates her vision, and the emphasis on the upper zone represents imagination.

Early in her relationship with John, Jackie cleverly became a social and intellectual resource to him. When he was hospitalized and recuperating from Addison's disease and back problems caused by his service in World War II, Jackie provided valuable research assistance for her husband's literary and political projects.

Jackie was raised in a world of high standards, protocol, social status, and decorum—she never forgot this background and tried to instill these qualities in her children, in both their choice of careers and their values. In fact, Jackie's greatest achievement was not her fame but her offspring. In the wake of her death, her son, John Kennedy Jr., emerged as the popular face of the Kennedys, until his untimely death in a plane crash. Her remaining child, Caroline Kennedy Schlossberg, is a bright, respected writer, lawyer, and education advocate.

PEN POINT   Is Handwriting Inherited?

Handwriting is not inherited, but behavioral traits can be. A parent and child or two siblings, with similar personalities or temperaments, can show remarkably similar handwriting traits.

A child may demonstrate his or her admiration or emulation of a parent by mimicking or imitating traits and/or handwriting. One can consciously alter one's writing to resemble another's, or unconsciously duplicate another family member's writing style.

Since handwriting reflects one's internal landscape and emotions, it is indeed possible that family members with similar (and inherited) personality traits or quirks would show similar handwriting features. As we've just seen, there were some interesting similarities in the handwritings of Joseph Sr. and John Kennedy.

*   *   *

I haven't spoke to my mother-in-law for eighteen months—I don't like to interrupt her!

—SOUPY SALES

*   *   *

We Are Family: Your Family's Handwriting Tree

It can be helpful and eye-opening to see what is revealed by the easily accessible greeting card notes, shopping lists, school notebooks, and phone messages your family members write. So why not create a family tree and then collect and review writing samples of family members and see who gets along with whom, who's a loner, who's stubborn, and who's your best ally?

What You Need

- Big sheet of paper
- Handwriting samples from family members
- Pencil or pen
- Ruler or straightedge
- Patience and insight

What to Do

- Create a rough genealogy chart or family tree that includes the members of your immediate family. Be sure to use a large sheet of paper or several sheets. You can use the sample here as a template, but be sure to leave lots of room—you're going to want to insert comments next to each member's name.

- Gather as many handwriting samples as you can from immediate family members or those with whom you regularly interact. Keep a lookout for letters and cards, notes, signed documents, old homework assignments, address labels, discarded faxes—anything you can find that is handwritten and directed to you or your immediate family. If you can't find any sample, ask!

- Once you've collected your samples, photocopy or replicate the Graphological Worksheet at the end of the book and

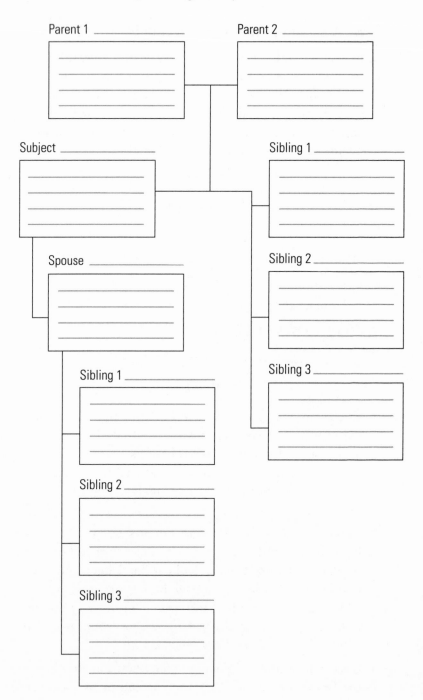

start recording traits and decoding the meanings. What buried treasures of insight have you uncovered?

- Now that you've come to some conclusions about each family member, record the key "personality points" on your family tree sheet, next to people's names, with the date. You should be able to start seeing fascinating dynamics emerging among various family members as you write. These patterns should help you better understand why you get along well with one of your brothers but not the other, or why your daughter is close with your mother but not with your husband's mother.

- Keep notes about who is most apt to get along with whom, and who is likely to be most difficult to get along with in general. If there's a "black sheep" in your family, see if his or her handwriting can give you clues about why.

- Always keep your collection of family members' writing samples on file, and add to it when you can. You'll find it enlightening to have samples from a period of time, because you will be able to see changes taking place in the lives and emotions of others. Maybe your "tough guy" brother will soften when a new and special girlfriend enters his life. Or you'll be able to see a "red flag" in your mom's writing that will enable you to relate to her with a bit more patience and understanding than before.

A collection of family handwriting samples is like a pictorial diary that you will come to treasure. You can also save it for your children and grandchildren so that they can learn more about the family as well. Remember, handwriting, unlike e-mail, is a living form of energy on the page. You can also collect samples over time to record changes and evolution in the lives of your family members.

And finally, while it's the rare family who resembles the happy and harmonious wholesomeness of a 1950s sitcom, with a bit of graphological insight you'll be better equipped to understand your relatives, recognize their potential, and, we hope, accept—or at least tolerate or overlook—their idiosyncrasies. Having this visual information handy affords you the opportunity to have stronger, healthier relationships with your loved ones and, with practice, lets you see potential areas of conflict so that you can better deal with them or detach from them. Since our families are here to stay, we may as well do our best to get along!

PEN POINT   Dearly Departed . . .

Now that you're learning how to better understand your family dynamics, why stop there? Maybe you've heard tales about Great-Grandpa Bill, who killed a bear with his bare hands, or Great-Great Grandma Lillie, who was a chambermaid to Queen Victoria—maybe you've even seen some old sepia prints of these family legends and wondered about them. If you're lucky enough to have samples of their writing (on a letter or a will or a deed), you can learn even more about who they really were. What a fascinating way to hone your skills and bring your ancestral past to life!

Graphological Advice on Family Issues

In my practice as a professional graphologist and executive coach, I'm often asked to help clients to resolve personality issues with other people. Family problems are the ones I hear about most frequently. Some clients have even started calling me the Dear Abby of graphology!

I'd like to share with you a selection of common family problems that I have been presented with in the hope that you will not only see how the solutions were derived but learn a little more about how you too can use graphology to resolve conflicts.

Do any of these scenarios sound familiar to you?

*   *   *

Dear Arlyn,

My mother will not accept my girlfriends. Every time I bring a woman home my mother manages to find fault with my choice. I've come close to getting engaged several times but backed away because no one ever seems to live up to my mother's standards. It's important to me that my mother like the woman I want to share my life with. At this point, I fear I'm destined to be single forever. What can I do?

—ALWAYS A BEST MAN, NEVER A BRIDEGROOM

Dear Never a Bridegroom,

Where do we see the problem in your mother's writing? The connection is very angular. If you look closely at the writing pattern, you see someone who is extremely difficult to influence. Her letters are overconnected and her placement of words on the page is crowded, revealing her need to interfere in the lives of others. We can infer from this that once she makes up her mind, it's hard for her to change it.

Why does she find fault with these women, and will she continue to do so? People who have this writing style are very narcissistic, competitive, and want to be the queen bee. They feel threatened by the women their sons love, because they fear that their role will be diminished.

This recurrent and insatiable need likely comes, unfortunately, from your mother's lack of emotional fulfillment, as evidenced by her disturbed lower zone. She is totally wrapped up in herself and therefore incapable of acknowledging the needs of others. This is confirmed by the size of letters and space patterns.

Because your mother has not been capable of fulfilling her own needs, she is looking to you to do this for her. Unfortunately, you cannot take on this responsibility, especially at the sacrifice of your own happiness. Try to pursue your love relationships and not allow your mother either to offer or withhold her approval. You alone can determine who is truly right for you. If you acquiesce to your mother's opinions, you run the risk of becoming the prisoner of a woman who will always find fault with your companions.

It is likely that in time—perhaps with the arrival of grandchildren—your mother will come around. Anything that enhances her image will work to everyone's benefit. And nothing makes a woman prouder than bragging about her grandchildren!

* * *

Dear Arlyn,

My husband spends a great deal of time with his seventeen-year-old daughter from his previous marriage and I feel very excluded. They've always been close, which is wonderful, but she seems to have no interest in a relationship with me. I'd like us to be more of a family when we're all together, so that I'm not an outsider. Anything I can do?

—STEPPED-OVER STEPMOM

Teaching sometimes drains
me of energy and patience
and understanding. It's
at this time that I need
human warmth & time
to sleep to restore my
strength.

My stamina is good. But,
when my schedule is very
busy with little let-up as
it was not long ago, my
nerves become raw and
I need enormous amounts
of sleep . . . and no addition
stress.

Dear Step,

Why does your stepdaughter ignore you? The middle zone of her writing sample reflects self-involvement and a general lack of development and maturity. This often reveals a need to be "Daddy's little girl."

This is an "oral" writing, as seen by the roundness of the letters, which could mean she did not get her verbal needs met as a young child. Communication, therefore, has become very important to her.

The writing is also sensual. Her father is a "safe male," therefore she may be reluctant to give him up. He is also the first man in her life to define her as a woman. His recognition and acknowledgment therefore become paramount to her.

Your stepdaughter may not want to grow up because she feels rewarded for being Daddy's little girl. She may not want to share her father.

Enjoy your own relationship with your husband and be secure enough in it to allow him his private time with his daughter. Praise and acknowledge her if you can for what you believe to be her attractive qualities. It is also important to understand better the relationship she had, or has, with her own mother.

Discuss your feelings with your husband. If you have a sincere desire to get to know his daughter better, he will only be pleased. Try to arrange private time with her. Suggest outings and activities unique to the two of you. Take her shopping, catch a movie, or have a day of beauty together. If you feel there is no progress over a sufficient period of time, the issues may be deeper and more complex, and best handled by a family therapist.

Also keep in mind that you may not be able to connect with your stepdaughter at this time in her growth and development. Relationships are often cyclical, so be patient. With time, sincerity, and sensitivity, she may come around. But if she doesn't, do enlist your husband's help or some counseling, because you don't want this relationship to affect your marriage negatively.

*   *   *

Dear Arlyn,

My husband has been having an affair with another woman for the past ten months. We have been married for ten years, have two children, and I am expecting a third. I am devastated! When I confronted my husband and threatened to leave him, he promised to change. In my current situation, I cannot work or afford a lawyer. Should I wait this out to see if it is a passing phase, or borrow money from friends and seek a divorce?

—Betrayed, Barefoot, and Pregnant

Could you please analyze this for me. This is a very emotional time for me.

I would like to take away the suggestion of over emotional to avoid over reacting

Dear Betrayed:

Let's look at the writing: Your husband is a man who has difficulty with fidelity. Highly impulsive, his letters are changeable with a strong right slant. While the writing looks charming, it reveals that he finds it difficult not to yield to his impulsive nature. He may promise to change, and no doubt mean it at the moment, but later on succumb to temptation.

Your husband hates to be told what to do. Notice that he writes off the line, which, in effect, is a boundary he ignores. This signals rebelliousness. He has a lot of unreleased anger, which is illustrated by angles in the lower zone, so he acts out his anger indirectly and passively by promising and then reneging on his promises. He is very caught up in his own needs.

My advice to you is to give him an ultimatum. Tell him you accept his promise to be faithful but want you both to seek marriage counseling. Give it another six months and see what happens. In the meantime, you should also consult with a lawyer to find out what your rights are given the length of your marriage, the size of your family, your husband's earning power, and divorce laws in your state. This information will help you to determine your plan of action and the consequences you both face if your husband cannot change. I wish you well!

*   *   *

Dear Arlyn,

I am married to a bright, interesting man who is retired. This is his second marriage and my first. Although my husband is on a pension, he indulges his children beyond reason. His children are in their late teens and early twenties, and they keep coming to him for money for tuition, expenses, hobbies, et cetera. I think they are taking advantage of him. Our marriage would be perfect if it wasn't for this problem. When I've pointed out that the children are taking advantage of him, my husband becomes iritated and then aloof. What should I do?

—Exasperated

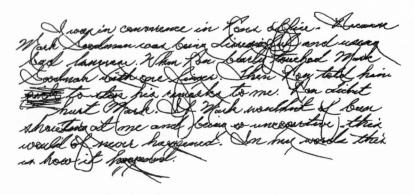

Dear Exasperated,

This is the handwriting of a person lost in his own illusions. He lives according to the dictates of his fantasy life and doesn't want to acknowledge or change his habits. If you look carefully, you will see the writing pattern leaves no room for anyone but himself. The space picture is very poor, making it difficult for him to deal with another's needs.

It is not uncommon for parents—particularly fathers—to show their love and support of their children monetarily, especially if they feel guilty about having divorced the children's mother or feel they are not adept at giving much emotionally. Your husband is simply "giving" to his children in the only way he knows how. And while they may indeed take advantage of his generosity, your husband seems comfortable with the arrangement, most likely because it alleviates his guilt. Unfortunately, there's not much you can do to change his feelings or relationship with his children, and though they're troublesome to you, the behavior patterns are so long-standing they are unlikely to change. This is a common problem in households where the husband or wife has children from a previous marriage—you are not alone!

Is the money your husband gives his children profoundly affecting your present and future lifestyle? If so, perhaps you need to discuss with your husband ways to balance your cash flow so that you can both cover your household expenses, enjoy your life together, and still find enough for his kids. Don't criticize how he handles things but instead provide ways in which everyone's needs can be met on a pension.

You say that your husband is bright and interesting—that's an important factor that should motivate you to work things out. If you're really concerned about the money and your husband is unwilling to discuss this with you, you have two choices: you can find ways to supplement your own income so that you have some financial control, or you can seek professional guidance for a solution.

*　　*　　*

Dear Arlyn:

My daughter-in-law and I don't get along very well and she criticizes me whenever we are together. I love my grandchildren and want to be a part of their lives, but my daughter-in-law makes it difficult—she is also overprotective and doesn't allow them to spend time alone with me, like other grandparents enjoy. The situation is hurtful and becoming unbearable. Do you think I should just remove myself from the family?

—HEARTBROKEN GRANDMA

*So wanted to see you as I whizzed
Through NYC. The only time was between
buses @ Port Authority and after having
just ridden Through town on a Greyhound,
I wouldn't ask anyone to do that for me —
especially not a friend! Had the
great pleasure of meeting
(asked her to give you a hug from me;
hope she does). Think of you lots - we'll
meet again - Work awaits!*

Dear Heartbroken:

Your daughter-in-law's writing connection is angular, rigid, and uncompromising. The letters are creatively written (note the t-h connection throughout), indicating intelligence, which makes her even more difficult to deal with. In addition, she is indeed possessive, as you can see in the rigidity and connections of the writing style. It is hard for her to let go.

Continue to attempt to form some kind of relationship with your grandchildren, and hope that when they get older they will discover you on their own, without the interference, shadow, and bias of their mother. Perhaps you can make an appeal to your son to help ease the relationship as well.

Simultaneously, you might want to reach out in a positive way to your nieces, nephews, or a friend's children or grandchildren. Or if you have strong, unfulfilled maternal instinct and love animals, you might consider adopting a pet with which you can form an attachment. (After the death of her husband, the syndicated columnist Cindy Adams found comfort with her Yorkshire terrier, Jazzy!)

Do realize, however, that the greater your need is for your grandchildren, the more power you give their mother. Your daughter-in-law's writing is very forceful, so there will be resistance. She no doubt enjoys the power of withholding. It is a large writing. Look at the middle zone—your daughter-in-law does not question either her judgment or decisions because she is self-involved.

The writing is quick, bright, and aggressive—she keeps plowing ahead. The space picture indicates that she doesn't want to know herself or learn from past mistakes. As she is unlikely to change her ways, you're going to have to change your expectations. Try not to make waves with her. Bite your tongue when you're around her—this is tough, but your love for your grandchildren will help you through it.

*   *   *

Dear Arlyn:

I have two children who are highly competitive. It is always a conflict of one-upsmanship, probably exacerbated by the fact that my daughter is fawned over by my husband to the despair of her brother. What can I do to help put an end to this rivalry, once and for all?

—Truce or Consequences

P.S. Just so you know, both my children are in their early thirties. This rivalry has been going on since childhood!

When I first got up Tracie made me a cup of coffee, and two english muffins. She talked about her conversation with mother and with Toni. Then she got ready for work and showed me how to get to your office.

On the way over the cab driver started in the wrong direction and wanted to charge me for it. I told him to turn around and restart the meter. He agreed

Son's

How's everything been this week? Things are going okay for me — not great but not too bad either. I've been exercising dilligently and going to Weight Watchers trying to create the "body beautiful!"

I hope this is enough handwriting. for now.

Daughter's

Dear Truce:

In reviewing the two letters you submitted, I see you have two gifted children. Your daughter's writing pattern is sophisticated, quick, purposeful, and efficient. I can see how she can readily engage others, stimulate and delight them with her personality. Her writing connections are original and at the same time highly simplified—a sure sign of an achiever.

Life—and meeting goals—comes easily and appears effortless for her. No doubt this charisma and competence represent a great challenge for your son by comparison. He has a different but equally impressive set of character traits. His angular writing shows a relentless need to achieve his objectives. This is also seen in his highly connected letters. The meticulousness and legibility of the writing show he is slower to process information than your daughter is but equally effective and competent. His writing also shows his perfectionism and sense of responsibility to do his work well.

It's hard to say no to your son, for he will not accept rejection easily in his professional life. However, he is probably aware that he lacks the sparkle and charisma of his sister. His writing is more workmanlike.

You should speak with your daughter and explain to her your son's problems and frustrations. Only she can have the maturity and self-confidence to give up the need to compete with and instead complement him. She is a fine person whose gifts permit her to be more generous. Much is given to her and, therefore, much is expected. If she realizes the impact of her behavior both on your son and on you, we can hope she will gain insight and change her attitude.

You must also find ways to show your appreciation of your son. His writing shows—by the overconnection of his letters and movement to the right—the qualities of a super salesman who is persuasive, hardworking, and respectable. Respect is as important as affection.

*　　*　　*

Dear Arlyn:

I am the parent of a teenage girl who is driving me to drink! She daydreams, has a room filled with pictures of film idols (hoping one day to be one of them), and binges on food when she becomes frustrated. She makes all kinds of excuses to avoid doing her chores at home or her assignments for school. We quarrel constantly and to no avail.

How can I better understand and get along with her? I'm too old to run away from home!

—Bothered and Bewildered

> I had my first day of school today and it went OK. I think my classes will be interesting. So I forgot what I was going to say
> Oh now I remember; psychologists analyze patients renderings of drawings of their parents. My favorite color is pink and I really love to babysit
> That's it
> I'm outta here

Dear Bothered,

Don't pack your suitcase just yet! Your daughter's writing is heavily focused on the middle zone, which indicates self-involvement. This is certainly a challenge for most parents.

It appears your daughter wants to escape the demands and responsibilities of her life by entering into a world of fantasy, where she will be rescued, taken care of, and most of all, validated. As we know, eating can often represent a feeling of comfort and release. Her writing also reflects a tendency toward perfection. People with this writing style need emotional gratification and look for fulfillment through food, daydreams, and fantasy.

My advice is to introduce her to an opportunity to use her skills in ways in which she can get back what she gives. Her writing is rounded, slow, deliberate, and legible. The rounded letters reveal warmth and a need for nurturing. This need can be fulfilled by encouraging her to do volunteer work with young children or at an animal shelter. Working with children or animals would allow her to give and receive affection and acceptance.

The light pressure of her writing suggests sensitivity to others. She is basically a gentle creature who belongs in non-threatening situations where she can thrive. In such a setting, she might be more motivated to take responsibility for her chores and schoolwork.

Criticizing and arguing with your daughter will only confirm her need to escape. The best way to deal with her is to acknowledge her struggle and make her feel that you have a genuine interest in her problems and in her.

CHAPTER 8

Trouble at Hand?

✳ ✳ ✳

HOW TO SPOT WARNING SIGNS IN HANDWRITING

*I hope by now you have begun to see that graphology
is an accurate method of uncovering personality traits
and hidden potential. As we know, appearances are not always
what they seem. This chapter explores the potential "dark side"
of personality. Whom can you trust? Who is not really who he or she
appears to be? How can graphology help you to deal with difficult
people? This chapter will show you how to detect warning signs
in handwriting: insincerity, deception, emotional detachment,
ticking time bombs, and other negative or problematic issues.
With this knowledge, you can see the "red flags" and take
heed before entering into a troubled relationship. Once
recognized, consult with a psychologist or professional
whose training can offer you guidance.*

Who knows what evil lurks in the hearts of men?

—OPENING LINE TO THE CLASSIC RADIO SERIES
THE SHADOW

ONE OF THE WAYS that handwriting analysis can be of help to you
in your personal or professional relationships is by alerting you to
potential "red flags" in someone's personality.

Though you're apt to find some negative or questionable traits
in every handwriting sample you review, an abundance or combination of problematic traits can be a warning sign. Handwriting
analysis shows character and potential; not every human being

will manifest his "dark side." While our DNA might signal a genetic predisposition for a particular illness or condition (like allergies, diabetes, cancer, and so on), this isn't a guarantee that we will be afflicted with this illness. Much depends on our environment, how well we take care of our general health, and the resources available to help prevent the onset of an illness.

By examining someone's handwriting, we're able to see both positive and negative tendencies, character traits, and potentials. This does not mean that the writer will always manifest these traits, but it certainly allows us to understand hidden problems that might appear and provide insight into dealing with a particular individual.

Please note: If you do get a writing sample that shows negative or questionable traits, check to see if this person was ill, under duress, or taking any type of medication. Handwriting quality is usually altered under such circumstances. Try to obtain a second sample after a passage of time, so that you can compare the writings to see if there are any changes.

Typical Warning Signs in Handwriting

In previous chapters we have looked at the positive and challenging aspects found in handwriting. Now we'll focus specifically on those traits that could be potential danger signals.

Dishonesty and Insincerity

- Cover strokes
- Poor rhythmic pattern
- Slow writing speed
- Ovals that contain double or triple loops or stabs through them
- Crooked writing
- Extreme left trend
- Capital letters in the middle of words
- Omission of letters or distorted letters
- Extreme rigidity or slackness

Violent Tendencies

- Disturbed rhythm
- Very heavy or uneven pressure
- Extreme right slant
- Muddiness
- Stabbing strokes
- Harpoons

Anger and Aggression

- Angles
- Club strokes
- Excessive or uneven pressure
- Letters getting larger at ends of words
- Uneven spaces between letters
- Mixed slant
- T-bars slanting downward
- Wavy baseline
- Sudden stops in movement

PEN POINT   Warning Signs in Writing

- Right margin wider than the left.
- Omitting essential words or parts of essential words
- Change in pressure and ink discharge in a stroke or line
- Muddy, pasty letters
- Tremors in the writing
- Disturbed rhythm
- Lack of or uneven pressure
- Marked discrepancy between the signature and the text
- Many corrections, retracing or reconnecting of letters
- Signature with several lines under it or a line through it

- Extreme left slant
- Strange or unnatural forms of i-dots
- Extremely slow or fast writing
- "Persona" or artificial writing
- If writing on lined paper, ignoring the lines or margins

Addictive Tendencies

- Slackness of the letterforms
- Neglect in form, particularly in the middle zone
- Uneven or large right margins
- Lack of or rigidity of movement
- Thread connection without pressure

Melancholia or Low Moods

- Rounded letters
- Connections between letters made lower toward the baseline
- Baseline that slants down (it can also go up if attempting to fend off depression)
- Weak or uneven pressure
- Slow movement
- Slackness

Compulsiveness

- Rigid, upright, overconnected form
- Slow and meticulous writing
- Strong pressure
- Arcade connections
- Small spaces between words
- Restricted writing; no release

Unconventional Sexual Expression

- Disturbed forms or movement in the lower zone
- Counterstrokes or angles in the lower zone
- Constricted writing
- Confused, tangled lines

*   *   *

Insane people are always sure that they are fine.
It is only the sane people who are willing to admit that
they are crazy.

—NORA EPHRON

*   *   *

The Dark, Notorious, and Infamous

Let's see what problematic behaviors or issues can be detected in the handwriting of a variety of famous, historic, or newsworthy people whose dark sides are well known.

TIMOTHY MCVEIGH:
Oklahoma City Bomber

Timothy McVeigh was a man of contradictions. His volatility, temper, and irritability can be seen in the abrupt halts at the ends of words. These qualities are underscored by the sharp leftward slant of the letters as well as the angles in the lower zone going toward the left, particularly in the letter *g*. The left slant also shows extreme resistance against anything McVeigh regarded as authoritative. His attitude toward authority was arbitrary, and he would rebel against it.

The letter *y* is deformed, with little hooks in the lower zone (note the words *any* and *body* in the second sentence), which signals difficulty in dealing with emotions and unconscious impulses. McVeigh handled his feelings inappropriately. The wide spaces between his words signify that he was a loner who had difficulty dealing with interpersonal relationships. He was isolated and alienated and not easy to know. Sudden changes in the writing's slant attest to considerable irritability and temper.

There is no sense of conformity in McVeigh's writing. Though it shows originality, this writing reflects someone who did not accept limitations or rules. He wouldn't even obey the accepted rules in handwriting, as shown in the way many of his letters move in the wrong direction.

What are the other warning signs in this handwriting? Notice the form, movement, and space. The form is primitive, with disconnected letters, indicating lack of integration as a person. The rhythm is poor, indicating poor discharge of energy. The movement to the left shows a return to the self, rather than to others. The small size shows suspicion and distrust.

In summary, McVeigh's anger, confused values, and rebellion are seen in the backward slant of his letters. The threading out of the letters in the middle zone shows his lack of confidence and refusal to respect boundaries and rules. The writing is dry, devoid of warmth and emotion, and the spaces between his words reveal his alienation from people and society at large.

ADOLF HITLER:
The Ultimate Dictator

Adolf Hitler's writing is rigid, angular, and aggressive. The strong right slant shows that, although he was an introvert, he was able to engage and connect with the German people.

The right margin reveals poor judgment. The letters collapse suddenly as he realized that he was at the edge of the page. If you look carefully, you will see that he refused to alter the line or interrupt it, so the words simply drop down. He was obsessive and compulsive, so obsessive, in fact, that rather than break up the word moving to the next line, he tried to go through the page barrier. This is driven writing. And, as you can see so graphically, once he got on a track, he couldn't get off.

This writing is actually Hitler's will, made in 1938—a messy writing filled with sudden disruptions. The danger signals in this writing are in its rigidity, angularity, intensity, and strong pressure. It is chilling.

In the fourth line down, look at the extreme right slant of the writing and the Sacre Coeur *m*, which reveals his lack of flexibility. Hitler could reach a fevered pitch when rabble-rousing, yet he was an inspired speaker.

Not only is the writing angular but it also reveals that Hitler was disdainful of boundaries—he refused to respect or obey margins. He didn't have to write this way; he just didn't want to obey the rules.

Hitler forced himself into a pattern no matter what, with extremely driven movement to the right. This writing pattern is sinister in appearance, with a poor space picture, broken margins, inappropriate breaks, and a sense of relentlessness. In fact, the connectedness and obsessiveness make each paragraph look like one sentence.

The rigidity in thinking, behaving, and emotional response is coupled with his rage, shown in the extreme angularity of the writing. Hitler's writing also goes into the lower zone as a further expression of anger and rage—a drive into the dark recesses of his personality. The extreme right slant confirms his need to connect with and engage others—get his message across and move toward his goals. The angles in the writing are like a military march; it is his way or no way.

The Führer could sweep others away with his crazy logic; his stroke is strong, intense, and compelling. His control starts to break when we see the letters in the right margin slope down into the lower zone. That slope is also echoed in his signature.

The overconnection of letters confirms his own brand of logic. No interference between lines and relatively good space picture testify to his competence.

Hitler's signature itself falls over—as if from a blow—penetrating the lower zone, which represents his darkest fantasies. It's an early forewarning of his suicide when his grandiose fantasies could not be realized. Failure was unacceptable to Hitler, and colliding with a reality he could not control was a humiliation he could not bear.

Susan Smith:
A Woman Without Compromise

Although she ultimately confessed to and was convicted of the drowning of her two small children in the car she pushed into a lake, Susan Smith's writing does not immediately signal the traits of a killer.

Note the extreme rigidity of Smith's letters, as well as their lack of connection. The lack of integration of the letters, coupled with their inflexibility, prevent her from having any capacity to adapt to extreme stress. As you may remember, Smith fell in love with a man who did not want to take on the "baggage" of her children. This is the writing of a woman with tunnel vision, fixated on one single idea, one single need. She lost all perspective on the world around her, and her stress unhinged her capacity to cope.

Smith's behavior and her subsequent view of the world have been filtered through the satisfaction of this need. The narrowness of the letters and their upright position confirm her inflexible temperament. The strong left slant of the letters and their precise form show she is a perfectionist, and this prevents her from considering and creating other choices or ways to adapt.

Although Smith was an adult at the time of the writing, the form level resembles that of a teenager. Like an adolescent, she prefers to draw the symbol of a heart instead of writing the word *heart*.

Smith committed the most unspeakable act and broke the most profound and sacred trust: that of the love of a mother for her children.

CHARLES MANSON

Did you get my letter — ?
Did you runget Lyn Fromme?
are you gone call me a boy from
the wash post + then come from
the Journal + ask me white ? why
don't you start with a woman's
point of View — the last
intrum took 4 years to line
up — there is much more
to this world of mine than
Nixon could hold — what
makes you think your life
style gets you left —

In this writing sample from Charles Manson, rhythm, space, form, and movement are extremely disturbed. The forms are neglected—a sign of someone who cannot be trusted. This looks like the writing of a loose cannon, a coil about to spring.

The intensity and mixed slant and the size of the letters vary in both direction and shape, revealing his instability. The t-bars are long, indicating his need for communication.

The left margin is completely undifferentiated, while the right margin is highly irregular. This shows that Manson was not interested in social norms. The left margin, which represents interest in learning and acquisition of culture, is very primitive and uneven.

The writing pattern is extremely troubling, particularly in the lower zone, suggesting that he had bad dreams and dark fantasies. The pressure is intense. It looks like he is having a temper tantrum on the page.

This writing shows a ticking time bomb, with sudden stops and angles that represent irritability and temper. There are hidden hooks. Look at the *y* in the word *you* in the first line.

In addition, in the sixth line from the bottom, in the word *intern,* there is an aggressive lead-in hook—this is called a claw, an ominous form in handwriting, violent, and hoarding. Manson was like a cobra—with no conscience—and so mean he could steal a dead fly from a blind spider. The letters are overly connected, showing obsessiveness. You can also see the claw in the words *hold* and *style.*

This is the writing of one who had both an unstable identity and disturbed sexuality, as evidenced by the troubling lower zone forms.

The signature is completely opaque and elaborate; the swirling lines keep it cleverly hidden—he didn't want you to see him as he really was. Why, one wonders, did he become a leader of a cult? The sheer force of his aggression, hostility, and perverse logic could have been quite seductive to followers who felt marginalized and misplaced.

The threadiness and neglect of form confirm his manipulative streak. The first sentence, "Did you get my letter?" is neglected;

nothing is clear. The lower zone forms all drift over to the left, representing the past, the search for a mother, no doubt signifying the nurturing he never received.

Finally, if you study the signature carefully, you will see the design of the Nazi swastika superimposed on it—possibly to emphasize Manson's commitment to a dictatorial fantasy.

KURT COBAIN
Suicide as Nirvana

> drug use is escapism whether you want to admit it or not.
> a person may have spent months, years trying to get help — but
> the amount of time one spends trying to set help and the years it
> takes to become completely drug free is nothing in comparison.
> every junkie ive ever met has fought with it at least 5 years and
> most end up fighting for about 15 25 years until finally
> they have to resort to becoming a slave to another drug the 12 step
> program which is in itself another drug /religion. If it works for
> you do it. If your ego is too big start at square one and
> go the psychological rehabilitate way. either way youve got
> at least 5 to 10 years of battle ahead of you.

With the recent publication of his handwritten diaries, Kurt Cobain, the late, lead singer of alternative rock band Nirvana, has become a fascinating subject. In this sample, we see fast, primitive, and underdeveloped writing. It reveals intelligence but is also disturbed. The space between the words, particularly at the top of the sample, is uneven and narrow.

Cobain lacked objective self-awareness. Remembering that the page is the writer's world, you can see that he had difficulty in knowing where he fit in his world, or how to negotiate it. The zone emphasis is uneven, and everything is changeable—there are mixed slants.

In the third and fourth lines, the first *the* and the word *takes* vary in size. We can see that Cobain was quick and bright, and the initial connections have a lot of originality. However, he was seemingly lost in space.

The baseline is uneven, and its waviness is particularly pronounced toward the bottom of the sample, indicating moodiness and mood swings.

Cobain's suicide was poignant because he was intellectually developed but emotionally suspended in early childhood.

RICHARD NIXON:
A Study in Signatures

President Richard Nixon was hardly a man of self-reflection. He truly believed he had no bad traits, and constantly justified his actions. As noted before, graphologists prefer to see more than one writing sample, because writing can change dramatically over time. Handwriting is truly an expression of our unconscious, and is therefore more a snapshot of the moment than a portrait. Let's see how this evolution applies in five samples by Richard Nixon.

1968

1969

1974

Late 1974

1968

When President Nixon took office, his writing pattern was confident and clear, showing that he took his time with matters of importance and was attentive to details. The pressure of the writing is good, signifying energy. The way the *x* in *Nixon* is executed (brought from the upper into the lower zone) represents creativity, aspiration, and the ability to translate ideas into action. Nixon was at the top of his game at the time of this writing. The clarity and definition of letters, which show sense of expectation and readiness to meet challenges, also confirm his state of mind. Here is a man comfortable with himself, having achieved a twenty-year goal: the presidency.

1969

Antiwar demonstrations began in 1969. We can in this signaturesee that Nixon was starting to lose control; his world was beginning to spin away from him. There is an unraveling in the writing, as shown in the enlarged capital letters, which represent his narcissistic defenses. Nixon now had difficulty completing the upstroke of the *d* in *Richard*.

The middle zone is small, indicating that he felt threatened and that his sense of self was diminished. The cross of the *x* in *Nixon* is now smaller, a signal that he was experiencing difficulty translating his ideas into reality, represented by the middle zone. The letters have become attenuated, symbolizing the president's increased difficulty in realizing his goals. They are also narrower, with no detail.

1974

Under pressure from Watergate investigators, Nixon's writing pattern has deteriorated further here, with umbrella cover strokes surrounding both the initial letters, *R* and *N*. He was now very distracted and insecure, and the writing became neglected. It appears to be falling apart. (It is even possible that Nixon began drinking heavily at this time.)

There is no definition in the signature. Look at the cross of the *x* in *Nixon*. It has become wavy and tentative, and drifts to the left, signaling his need for reassurance and self-definition, and his movement is away from others.

Late 1974

This was the year Nixon resigned. He had lost everything: his confidence, self-esteem, and sense of direction. The writing shrinks into a flat line. There is a hook in his last name, seen as an attempt to dot the *i*. The i-dot in the upper zone is no longer a detail but has become almost a fantasy.

The cross of the *x* in *Nixon* now turns and curves, with nowhere to go. The writing has become a mere shell of itself.

Now, let's look at Nixon's writing as he started to rebuild his image from disgraced president to respected elder statesman.

1992

In a letter Nixon wrote in 1992, his signature now consists of his initials surrounded by a circle or protective cocoon. Look at the left margin: it becomes gradually wider. The left of the page represents the mother or the past, so it can be interpreted to mean that Nixon is running from his past.

Nixon could be called a tragic figure of our time because he had such extraordinary ideas and vision, as seen in the upper zone of these writing samples. But we see increasing difficulty in carrying these creative aspirations down into the middle zone of reality and making them work. Instead, his ego appears increasingly nonexistent. His need to impose himself upon the page prevented him from having any real understanding of the world around him. Although he began using an overinflated signature, it masked a fear of emptiness and a need for constant acknowledgment.

JOHN GOTTI

The interesting thing about John Gotti's writing is that it does not reflect one's preconceptions of a mobster. For example, in the second line from the bottom, in the word *wish*, we see a circle i-dot. There are also the large, oval exclamation points. These forms are very surprising in a man we perceive as macho. The writing, in fact, has several feminine characteristics, including soft pressure. His writing is basically school form. One might speculate that Gotti is using his machismo to cover up his sense of personal inadequacy. His writing, like his dress and general appearance, is somewhat dramatic.

Although the letters are neither developed nor original, there is a sense for form on the page, which corresponds to this interest in style. The legibility of letters is impressive. He is very concerned about how he appears to others. There is also a grace in the way he crosses his *t*'s. This is a form of elaboration, which draws further attention to himself.

However, Gotti does not allow enough space—there is no right or left margin, as the original sample extended to both margins of the page—which means there is no room for anyone else in his world. Yet, surprisingly, his signature is the same size as the text, showing a balance and perception between his self-image and how others see him.

The extensions in the words *health* and *letter* are his way of filling space, not letting others talk or get close to him. At the ends of these extensions, there are thickening club strokes, signifying cruelty. He is definitely unavailable.

This writing is basically cold, with very few breaks, and is somewhat overconnected. The warning signals are in the pronounced and angular lower zone. The margins represent a defensive wall that protects his vulnerability. The lower zone in the letter *f* has aggressive harpoons, which resemble wire hangers. This is the mark of the domestic tyrant, someone with a lot of hidden anger. The narrow margins extending almost to the end of the page are a safeguard against letting anyone else in and being vulnerable.

YASSER ARAFAT
Chairman of the Palestine Liberation Organization

Yasser Arafat's writing emphasizes the lower zone, not only in the letter *f,* but in the initial *A* in his last name. The letter *A* does not belong in the lower zone, but he has extended it there sharply, like a spear, indicating aggression. It further means he places importance on money and power.

Arafat underlines his name, which emphasizes his sense of identity. His signature is showy. Notice the end of the underline—there is a fishhook, which reveals tenacity.

The baseline moves upward, which, contrary to popular belief, does not signify high spirits but instead demonstrates the desire to appear more enthusiastic and secure than is truly felt. Arafat's signature shows duplicity; there will always be a hidden agenda. The underline also divides the signature in half, as if what is on top of the line is one identity, and what is below the line is someone else.

The signature is full of spikes and angles, making Arafat hard to read. This "persona writing" is full of artificial forms, indicating that it is not a spontaneous expression; it is contrived. As the Sufi proverb goes, "Put your trust in God, but keep your camels tied."

* * *

In conclusion, we live in an unprecedented time, when life has taken on great fragility and so many certainties and norms we take for granted are being called into question. There are unlimited possibilities for surprise, leaving us with a desire for information, control, and equilibrium.

Graphology provides a form of assessment that may offer unexpected clues to the mystery of another and can often help prevent unpleasant surprises.

CHAPTER 9

Dotting Your *I*'s and Crossing Your *T*'s

*   *   *

USING GRAPHOLOGY TO MAKE BETTER CHOICES

Now that you're more knowledgeable about the "language" of handwriting, this chapter will show how you can employ that knowledge to make more informed decisions. Using graphology, you'll learn how to choose the right home health care aide, doctor, lawyer, nanny, housekeeper, and financial planner; and how to assess the strengths and weaknesses of those who have influence and power in your life. Graphology can help you "look before you leap" into any situation.

OUR DAILY LIVES ARE FILLED WITH CHOICES: what to eat, what to wear, what presents to buy for loved ones, and whether to take an umbrella or a coat when the weather might turn. These are the easy choices. But then there are choices we make that involve others—who's the best doctor, the most responsible baby-sitter, which contractor is the most reliable, and so on. In making decisions about people who tend our health and household, or whose services we retain, first impressions can sometimes be misleading. References are helpful but may be scant. However, graphology can give you an extra assessment tool.

So the next time you're not sure which person is the most trustworthy choice, or if you have made a selection but want further confirmation, ask for a handwriting sample to review. You may be surprised at what is revealed, and that information will only help you make better decisions.

Whom Should You Choose?

By now you've come to see that handwriting shows an individual's character traits, strengths, weaknesses, and potentials. Once you learn more about a person through handwriting, you'll be able to see whether he or she is the best match for you. For example, a doctor might have fabulous credentials and glowing recommendations from patients, but his bedside manner may leave a lot to be desired. If you need a physician who is a great communicator and provides a lot of TLC, you might seek out another qualified physician who can also meet your more personal criteria.

Now you can use what you've learned throughout this book to influence your decision making, but keep in mind you should always get a professional opinion.

Here are a selection of people you might need to hire: home health aides, doctors, lawyers, nannies, housekeepers, contractors, and financial planners. Review the handwriting samples of each pair, being mindful of the qualities you would be most comfortable with, and note your choice in each. Then read the analyses to see how well you've assessed the writers' strengths and weaknesses and determine whether you made the right choice.

Who Would Be a Better Home Health Care Aide?

Review these two handwriting samples and decide which person would make a better home health care aide to look after dear old Grandpa, who is recovering from a broken hip and hates being a patient.

A

B

Recipes

Keto Turkey Stuffing Supreme
½ cup Butter' Done
1 Teaspoon garlic fresh Done
2 cup Fresh mushroom or 1.10 oz drained Done

Home Health Care Aide, Choice A

This sample shows a person with a strong work ethic who is a perfectionist, as seen by the care she takes in writing and the meticulous letter formations. The upright slant shows she is in control, accepts responsibilities, and does the right thing with grace. This is a good person. She does everything with precision; nothing is neglected.

The lower zone of the writing is not emphasized, so money is not her motivation; she is motivated by people (namely, her patients). She is nurturing, sensitive, reliable, and consistent. She is diligent, with a strong sense of duty and perseverance. The rounded forms, light pressure, and upright slant of the letters confirm this. The highly connected letters show that if she makes a promise, she will keep it. They also mean, however, that you cannot break a promise to her!

Home Health Care Aide, Choice B

The writing of this person is primitive and undeveloped. The connection is a mixture of sharp angularity and threads, with extremely poor rhythm. The word *mushrooms* contains several angles, which dissolve into negative threads. The base is so irregular that, when combined with the other writing traits, it shows deviousness—you don't know which way this person will turn. This is also a very negligent writing; the irregularity of the letters (which are often obscure) reflects potential problems with communication.

The writing drifts aimlessly, and each word that dips into the lower zone has a different formation. These traits indicate some personality problems and a lot of unpredictability. The writing pressure is strong, and if you look closely you can feel the writer's anger on the page—her words and letters are like little temper tantrums. This is not a person who is interested in others; she does as little as possible and would always make excuses to cover her mistakes. She would not make a trustworthy home health care aide.

Who Would Be a Better Doctor?

Review these two handwriting samples and decide which doctor you feel would provide you with the best and most personalized care.

A

B

Doctor, Choice A

This writing style is cold and emotionally undeveloped, as seen in the neglected form level and wide distances between words. This could pose a problem in the doctor's being able to relate sensitively to patients. The strokes are weak, which can indicate mood swings. However, this doctor is intelligent, and the connections are creative (like the *th* in the first word, *then;* the *a* into the *n* in the *and* on the third line; the *d* into the *t* in the words "did this"), so the issue is not credentials or intelligence but temperament and capacity for relationships.

There is laziness and self-indulgence in the writing, which can be seen by the threadiness and general space picture. This could mean he might not make extra effort to recommend a wider variety of options for his patients' health problems. This doctor will not likely be able to meet the needs of a demanding and informed patient.

Doctor, Choice B

This doctor's writing is well organized, and the space picture shows great insight and objectivity. He is also an exceptional diagnostician, which we can see in the arrangement of space on the page, indicating clarity of vision and understanding. The white space on the page shows that he leaves room for others, has sensitivity, and is a good listener. The hooks on the ends of strokes show his tenacity. He's highly intelligent yet exercises great care and neglects nothing. This sample does not represent typical doctors' writing, which is often illegible because of speed. Here the individual letters are clear—this writer wants his message to be understood.

See the *o*'s in the phrase "I hope to go" and in the word *loves* on the next line? Each of them is leaning to the left. This doctor knows what he wants and how to work to get it. The noticeable left slant shows he will follow the dictates of his principles, regardless of pressure. He is not going to be told what to do by others, and what he does, he does well. He has very high standards, which he will not compromise. Though this is an older doctor, his perception, as well as ability to process information easily, are those of a much younger man.

Who Would Be a Better Lawyer?

Review these two handwriting samples and decide which lawyer you would choose to help you with your legal needs. (This sample has been reduced for format.)

A

[handwriting sample A]

B

[handwriting sample B]

Lawyer, Choice A

This lawyer's writing is conservative. He will do what he promises and work hard to honor his responsibilities and obligations. The writing pattern is clear, well organized, and legible, and although the forms are narrow, the rhythm is impressive.

Though his writing is a bit school type in form, it moves with deliberate and careful letter formations and rhythmic momentum to the right. This shows that even though he is conservative, he is forward thinking. This sample was written on small notepaper, but the writing is well centered on the page, and he makes good use of the space. He's a very effective and competent lawyer. This is the writing of a perfectionist. Each *i* is dotted, *t* crossed. He is well prepared, as seen by the lead-in strokes prevalent in the left margin.

This is a smooth, active, and flowing writing, revealing one who knows how to set and reach his goals with ease, fluidity, and brilliance. There is strong rhythm and movement, yet despite the speed of his thinking, the letters are formed with great care, showing a commitment to detail and a respect for the reader. Lawyers, like doctors, often write quickly because their minds work faster than their hands. The time taken for legibility is impressive. In hiring this lawyer, you would choose a man who is thoughtful, careful, and honorable, one who leaves no detail to chance.

Lawyer, Choice B

The lower zone of this writing is going in the reverse direction. That is an immediate signal that this lawyer may not be as trustworthy as you would like him to be. He is not following the normal line or expectations, so he can hide and disguise things easily. This is a very rigid, controlled writing, and though this lawyer is capable and competent, he is after only his own interests. He is a compulsive man (seen in the overconnection of the letters), who finds it hard to let go of anything he believes he has earned, won, or is entitled to—he is territorial. This is a thinking type, and the writing is full of tension. Sudden changes of direction in the letters show the potential for irritability and unexpected outbursts of temper. The writing slant is mixed—sometimes upright, sometimes leaning to the left. This means he could suddenly change his approach. With this personality dynamic, he could do well in the courtroom, but you may never know where you stand with him as a client. He is highly intelligent but also a sophisticated exploiter.

The narrow letters and wide spaces between the words testify to his introversion. He keeps his own counsel. This is a left-slanted, cold writing; he has a tendency to move away from people and has a problem with authority. He is very precise, a perfectionist, and emotionally unavailable. Everything is on his terms. This lawyer will do as much or as little as he wishes. There is a lot of tension on the page, like a coil about to spring. He is very competitive and wants to win. His space pattern shows detachment from others' feelings. Although you may prefer someone aggressive to represent your interests, do realize that this lawyer will go his own way.

Who Would Be a Better Nanny?

Review these two handwriting samples and decide to which person you would entrust the care of your children.

A

> I will take care of your coffee mashine on Wed. I hope that's ok. with you I do certainly know to replace things that I brake - But In the Same time You should know that it was in

B

> I cry very very often Because it Hurts and I worry about the children all my children all over the World, I live for them.
> If a Man could SAY nothing AgAINST a character but what he can prove, HiSTORY cou

Nanny, Choice A

With unusually intelligent writing, this nanny could be considered "top of the line." Her intelligence permits her to understand both the requirements of the position and the needs of the people who employ her. This is a print script that is very upright but shows education and competence. The only concern you might have is that because of her high qualifications and sophistication, she may tire of tending to children and become interested in a more intellectually challenging position. But whatever she does, she will do extremely well. This is a form-conscious artistic writing, showing that she will take on her responsibilities with flair and style. Appreciation of her uniqueness, efforts, and effectiveness is very important to her.

The space picture in this sample is not that impressive because the writing is so large. The unclear space may indicate that she does not have good insight as to where to apply her talents. This nanny's letters are large but rounded and full of warmth and emotion. They also reveal her capacity for nurturing. She enjoys and needs the company of a bright and stimulating family environment. She will be selective about the people she works for. Once she makes that choice, however, she will be truly committed and use her creativity and sensitivity to improve the quality of life for the children she cares for as well as their parents.

Nanny, Choice B

If you chose the writer of this sample as a nanny, your nursery would be occupied by the eccentric music legend Michael Jackson!

Although this sample was written when Jackson was in his thirties, it could be by a teenager. Jackson mixes upper- and lower-case, which shows he is confused about himself. The movement, form, and space are weak and disturbed. The angularity represents his discipline, resilience, and determination. The lower zone throughout is very disturbed. The letters are narrow, which shows his introversion; the writing style is both slack and contracted, and the letters drift. A lack of development and immaturity are seen in the confusion of space and inconsistency in the size of the letters. The sloping baseline reveals his melancholy, disillusion, and loss of innocence. Jackson's level of education is low, and this sample is replete with spelling errors. The lack of punctuation and organization represents an almost free-association thought process. Antisocial behavior can be seen by his disregard for norms, even the norms of good grammar and correct spelling.

There's an irony in the slow, carefully written, legible writing. Jackson is a perfectionist, who wishes to communicate on his own terms, as unconventional and inappropriate though they may be. You would never guess that this writer, who is filled with passivity, apparent sadness, and lack of energy, is a renowned entertainer who spellbinds audiences. Fame, scandals, and gossip aside, you would not be likely to hire someone with such emotional conflicts and lack of maturity to care for your children.

Who Would Be a Better Housekeeper?

Review these two handwriting samples and decide which person you would choose to take care of your house and household errands.

A

> I am organized r responsible
> I take great pride in
> keeping homes beautiful,
> taking care of art and
> antiques.

B

> I think President Bush is wrong in trying to what it
> seems force the American People into war. It is
> obvious that most of the world is against it and his
> reasons are not enough to convince me that force is
> needed to resolve the problem with Iraq. Saddam
> is only as dangerous as we make him and war will only
> create more tyrants like him.
>
> I believe tough restrictions and constant control over
> Saddam is the only way to keep him at bay. Too
> many people will suffer and die because bush has a
> personal vendetta against Saddam. I hope more people
> will come together...

Housekeeper, Choice A

The writer of this sample is not a good choice as a housekeeper for several reasons. The writing pattern is disorganized with a large middle zone, which shows self-involvement. The slack letters indicate self-indulgence; laziness is shown in the neglect and un-evenness of the letters.

The writing form indicates a lack of discipline, revealing someone who can be impulsive—she may be prone to temptation, so keep your good jewelry hidden! The inappropriate size of some letters shows a confusion of values. The pressure is weak, revealing poor stamina and energy—there is very little discipline in the slant, so she can easily lose interest and enthusiasm for her work. Responsibility is something she runs from rather than welcomes.

*   *   *

I'm an excellent housekeeper. Whenever I leave a husband, I always keep his house.

—Zsa Zsa Gabor

*   *   *

Housekeeper, Choice B

This individual shows perfectionism and discipline in the upright-ness of the letterforms. This writer has integrity: there is clarity and ease in the letters and good space surrounding them. It is this space picture that indicates her good judgment. She sees what needs to be done, is organized, and will not push the boundaries of famil-iarity with her employer. There is no impulsiveness, slackness, or self-indulgence in the writing; the upright and carefully written letters are further testament to her integrity. The rigidity shows that once she gets fixed on a goal, she will not deviate from it.

There is a tending toward the left in some of this writing, which means that, although she has a fine character, there will be a period of adjustment in her tenure with you. In the word *reasons* (fourth line down), the final *s* is separate. This shows the writer is cautious and thinks before she acts. Overall, this candidate is in-telligent, organized, disciplined, and committed—a good choice for tending to your household.

Who Would Be a Better Contractor?

Review the two handwriting samples on the following page and decide which contractor you would hire to help you undertake a major renovation.

A

B

Contractor, Choice A

I sincerely hope you did not make this choice! This writing sample shows extreme harshness, and is replete with anger and aggression—not someone you'd want to have around your house for weeks or months! This is anal writing—you see that quality in the angularity of letters and in the strong pressure. There's a bit of thread, too. Threads and angles together can suggest duplicity and manipulation. The strokes, even the cross-outs, are very aggressive. The black lines obliterating words (which he considers mistakes) show his sensitivity to criticism. By the rigidity of the letters we can see that he insists on having his own way.

If written words could be heard, this sample would be screaming. This is a very angry guy. His resentment is sudden, dull, and thick, and works like acid. Nonetheless, this is a man who is smart and likely a financial success, as seen by the clever and expedient connections and speed and originality of his letter-forms. The combination of aggression and angularity in the writing, along with the pressure, bit of thread, and rigidity, shows his determination and unwillingness to do anything that doesn't fit into his scheme of things. For all these reasons you would find negotiating and working with this contractor very challenging.

Contractor, Choice B

The writer of this sample is a good choice, because he is a perfectionist. His writing is legible and meticulous. He wants everything to be clear and worked out in advance. He adheres to the lines, which means he understands rules and directions. The centered message on the page and the spaces between lines show he clearly understands the needs of others, is a good listener, and is willing to negotiate. The organized writing and absence of tangled lines means there is no hidden agenda with this man—what you see is what you get. Even though he has used a felt-tipped pen in the sample (which is known to make pastose strokes), the letters are not thick or smudgy—this shows care and consideration for the reader.

In conclusion, this man would make an utterly reliable and dependable contractor. Working with him would be a dream because he would be likely to keep all your plans and budgets and deliver his work to perfection.

Who Would Be a Better Financial Planner?

Review these two handwriting samples and decide which financial expert you feel would be most trustworthy.

A

The caveat here is that manager position sizes should be small with directional exposure in aggregate rolling up to be negligible.

B

Linda and I are so proud of both of you and look forward to seeing both of you in The White House. Hope you have a great Christmas with your family,

Warmest regards,

Financial Planner, Choice A

This writer is very smart as there are many simplifications in his script. The writing has precision yet a threadiness that shows flexibility and creativity. Look at the connection of the letters *t* and *h* in the words *the* and *that* and *with*. This shows he can see things clearly, quickly, and analytically (confirmed in the small size of the letters), and to make corrections when necessary. This precise writing reflects the candidate's competence. There is no roundness in the writing, so he is not apt to make emotional decisions; he values objectivity, independence, caution, and freedom of movement. The lack of roundness also means he makes decisions with detachment.

His mind works very fast and you can see this speed in his writing. He has a course of action and likes to stick to it. Although he processes information quickly, he is in no way irresponsible or reckless. He can readily see what is important and what's not, and is resolute in his judgments. Overall, this writing shows a sophistication and quickness that indicate a financial

planner who can seize a good opportunity or find overlooked possibilities that are innovative or unique and ultimately beneficial to
your portfolio.

*   *   *

*I go to a good accountant. He saves me time—five,
ten years!*

—MILTON BERLE

*   *   *

Financial Planner, Choice B

If you entrust your money to this individual, you're giving your
nest egg to Ken Lay, former CEO of Enron! Lay mixes upper and
lower cases, indicating duplicity. There is much variation in the
size of the letters and a lot of threadiness. In the first words, *Linda
and I,* the *a*'s are split. This form shows he is fast and shifty, able
to maneuver for his own purposes. In addition, the *a* in the word
are is smudgy. These are all signs of a disreputable character. The
d in the word *proud* is strange as well, another red flag.

In the sentence *You have a great Christmas,* the *a* goes into the
lower zone, where it doesn't belong, which represents a love of
money. This is the writing of someone who is comfortable with
changing everything; the size, slant, and form in the writing are
variable. Look at the *y*'s in the words *you* and *family*—the lower
zone moves to the extreme left, a sign of weakness and insecurity.
There is no structure to the writing. Many of the letters
throughout the sample drift aimlessly to the left—a sign that his
ego is in need of reinforcement.

The ambivalence and ambiguity of the letters show someone
who is hard to pin down and has no sense of accountability. This
is a deficit that is unacceptable in one who is given responsibility
for the investments of others.

*   *   *

Perhaps you are beginning to see why we call writing "body language on paper." Handwriting will display nuances of a person's character that you might not readily see in an initial meeting or well-coached interview. Graphology is another way to help you "look before you leap" into any relationship. When your health, family, or children's well-being is at stake or you entrust your care, money, or home to another, you want to know that she or he is someone you can trust and who can deliver. Today, because personal references are limited and often noncommittal, if you see questionable or negative signs in candidates' handwriting, you have the option of digging deeper into their background or consulting with a professional graphologist before making a commitment.

CHAPTER 10

Final Strokes

* * *

HONING YOUR CRAFT

*We've come to the end of the book, and this chapter will
wrap up with some questions and answers about graphology, one
last exercise to help you hone your craft, and contact information
to enable you to take your knowledge the "next step."*

*Our character is what we do when we think no one is
looking.*

—H. JACKSON BROWN JR.

YOU'VE COME A LONG WAY in your knowledge about handwriting analysis and how it can help reveal the character of others
and make you and your life more successful. This is not the end of
the book but rather the first step to greater awareness and the
foundation of your education in the field of graphology.

Frequently Asked Questions About Handwriting Analysis

My career as a professional graphologist takes me around the
world to lecture and consult, and I find that I am asked many
questions about my work and this profession in general. Here are
answers to some of those frequently asked questions.

Q. What is the difference between graphology and astrology?

A. Graphology doesn't involve your date of birth, the planets,
or the stars, and it doesn't predict the future, as astrology
claims to do. But it will predict how people can behave under
certain circumstances. Handwriting is a living part of a person

and his or her energy. Your handwriting is determined not by your hand but by your brain. Graphology is often considered a form of psychology, not an occult or New Age study.

Q. What types of companies hire graphologists?

A. Fortune 500 companies have been known to hire graphologists to match a manager to the right position. Private investigators hire graphologists to determine a person's integrity. Jewelry stores or gem distributors use graphologists when hiring people to handle expensive merchandise or money. Entrepreneurs hire graphologists to determine "secret agendas" before going into a negotiation.

Q. What is your training?

A. I was fortunate enough to be trained by one of the foremost proponents of Gestalt graphology in the United States, Felix Klein. Klein was highly experienced in graphology as well as in the psychology of handwriting, so I simultaneously learned about and applied the typology of personality concepts developed by Freud, Jung, and Adler.

In Europe graphology is often taught at the university level. A full course usually runs three years, and one must defend oneself before a panel of experts to receive a degree or certification. In the United States, various associations provide training in handwriting analysis, and you must adhere to the criteria of the association from which you are receiving your training. Often students have to defend their findings before a group of peers in order to conclude their coursework. Study of graphology in the United States usually takes one to three years.

Q. My handwriting changes all the time. Won't it be a problem for you to read the real me?

A. While it's true that your moods change daily, people recognize you walking down the street regardless of how you are feeling. It's the same with handwriting. The core of your writing should remain the same, even though the letters may be affected by your mood, fatigue, medication, or simply age. Handwriting is a snapshot of a moment in time, not a portrait, which is why it's important to have more than one sample to analyze.

Q. Why is graphology taken so seriously in Europe but isn't yet held in the same esteem here?

A. In Europe graphology has been taught at universities, often connected with departments of psychology. People who have other degrees (in neurology, social work, psychology, psychiatry, and so on) often want to enhance their knowledge by learning graphology. Because it has been part of the culture longer, graphology has serious applications in European businesses. And since the fall of communism, there has been a renewed interest in graphology throughout Eastern Europe. It's now filtering its way to the United States.

Q. If I read a book on graphology, can I call myself a graphologist?

A. No, absolutely not! You wouldn't call yourself a doctor based on reading one medical book, would you? Graphology is a serious discipline that takes a lot of study, knowledge of psychology and the human mind, and understanding of human nature. As in learning anything else, you must receive adequate hands-on experience along with study, discipline, and certification. You must also understand and abide by a code of ethics. This book can give you a start to a more serious pursuit of this fascinating subject.

Q. Do you as a graphologist have the power to determine people's careers?

A. No. By the time I see a candidate, it is likely that he or she has been interviewed, references received, and background checks complete—I'm only a portion of a lengthy process.

Q. Is graphology an art or a science?

A. It's actually both. It's a science in that it can be a predictor of behavior. Letters on a page are like a language, and graphology helps you learn to decode this language. It is also similar to many personality assessment tests given to help people find the right careers or jobs. But it can be a true art form in the manner by which you convey the information you have gathered to others. I have always been taught that you can only share with a person what she or he is able and ready to receive.

Q. Why is there so much misunderstanding surrounding graphology?

A. Because in the United States there is no national certification or license, no board or "bar" exam to pass to become a graphologist. Professions lacking these types of certifications come under more scrutiny and, hence, more criticism and misconceptions.

Q. Why is it difficult to interpret a child's or teenager's writing?

A. Our writing is not fully developed until the age of twenty-one. Before then we are in a stage of emotional and physical evolution, so there's great flexibility in the letters and how we handle a pen or even our hand. In fact, our handwriting can change even in our adult years. That's why it's so important to have a variety of samples from the same person when conducting an analysis.

Q. Why do you believe handwriting analysis works?

A. Writing is an unconscious part of us and can reveal a great deal more than one realizes. Over time, companies I consult for come to see its accuracy. I hope you have seen that through reading this book.

Trying Your Hand

Now that you have been introduced to the basics of handwriting analysis, you will have a chance to apply, assess, and enhance your knowledge. In this section, you will find six writing samples—choose as many as you wish to analyze. After you complete your analyses, read the analysis of each writer and check your findings.

You may wish to refer to earlier chapters to refresh your memory and utilize the Graphological Worksheet and Graphological Key at the end of this book.

1

2

The ability to read and write
is a skill which many take for granted.
Yet millions of children around the world
remain illiterate.

The joy children gain from reading
is incalculable. That is why education is
the top priority for my Government and why
I support this appeal by UNICEF. I hope
it will result in many more children
around the world sharing the pleasure of
reading, writing, and learning.

Tony Blair

3

THE WHITE HOUSE

September 10 = 1991

Dear Mr. Battaglia —

So many thanks for sending the absolutely lovely shawls. There is no question they are the finest - softest and nicest I or ever seen. In order to be able to accept such a glorious gift I am going to share them with my most precious daughters-in-law. So I am thanking you for all of us!

You said such nice things about my George. Thank you for

Barbara Bush

4

Our universe is but one fragment of a greater living Being. All of us exist as parts of this larger whole. If we can think of our existence in this way, we w be more inclined to acknowledge our responsibility to our planet, and our fell human beings. As members of the family of mankind we hope that each of us will take responsibility for all our actions that one will feel responsibility for the other. That the strong will extend a hand to those who are fragile. This is my dr we all need a dream to hold onto; to make us better than we are. Then the close of our brief time here, we can t we did our best; and that is no small +-

Mia Farrow

5

The outstanding quality of this person is his
ability to cope with situations outside the realm
of emotions. He was able to learn to deal with
all kinds of situations. It was not part of
his upbringing to learn that. This he had
to do under the most difficult cir —
cumstances. One of the difficulties was
his introversion. It prevented him (at least
in the beginning) to practice relationships
to other people, even if it only concerned
business. The sheer necessity of a business
man to relate to other people made it essential
for him to deal with people and learn how
to conduct himself in such given situations.
This was not an easy task for him. A lot
of the energy was consumed by this under-
taking. The energy that he possessed at
the time when he did go into business
was not the greatest. And so little of
the energy that remained was used

Felix Klein

Handwriting Samples Analyzed

1. *Ralph Lauren: Fashion Designer*   This is the writing of an
extrovert. Lauren is active and knows how to make his gifts of
intelligence, creativity, and aesthetics work to attain his
objectives. Look at the finals of the words *vision, achieved,*
and *power.* The stroke is smooth and reaches out to others as
well as to the next challenge. The small *hooks* at the ends of
these words show his tenacity.

In the upper zone of the signature, the capital letters are elaborate, indicating creative fantasy. The *R* and *L* are overwhelming in size when compared with the middle zone. The large capital letters draw attention to himself and let the public know who he is. *Ralph* and *Lauren* are equally graceful, and each name flutters at the end.

There are strong lead-in strokes in the *t*'s, which show Lauren's energy and enthusiasm. Many of these lead-ins are in the left margin and start at the baseline, and they provide extra energy and drive, which act as his "psychic caffeine" for the day.

The first letters of several words, such as *conviction, can,* and *energy,* are disproportionate to the rest of the letters; see also the *g* in *get* in the last line, which is larger than the *t*. The first letter on the page—*A*—and the *H* in *He* show graceful, artistic writing that is smooth and effective.

The long t-bars also confirm his ability to communicate what he wants to share. The finals get broader, which means he knows how to assert and affirm himself. The rhythm is graceful, and the writing is quick and elegant. The large letters and uneven size of the middle zone can serve as compensation for his insecurities and fuel his ambition. And the i-dots are high, showing Lauren's high standards. Lauren is a true original and a work in progress.

2. *Tony Blair: Prime Minister of the United Kingdom* This writing reflects a thinking typology. The space, movement, and form are all in balance, beautiful, and rhythmic, like musical notes. The t-bars move strongly move to the right, showing enthusiasm and a desire to reach goals and challenges.

The connection of the letters, particularly in *write* in the first line, *of* in the third line, *joy* in the fifth line, and *this* in the eighth line, show an extraordinary sophistication, creativity, and originality. They also demonstrate expediency, because Blair creates his own letter formations with speed and clarity.

There is brilliance on the page—the paraph under his signature comes to a hook that belies his tenacity. Even the *B* and the way it connects to the *l* in *Blair,* is witty and smooth. The signature is the largest form on the page, and the paraph under it puts further emphasis on his identity.

Now look at the word *support* (fourth line from bottom). The bottom of the initial *p* is written first, and its upper loop flows to the lower zone of the next *p;* the upper zone of that second *p* connects to the following letter, *o.* This is a light, delicate touch and offers more examples of Blair's originality and quickness of mind.

In the last line, the *g*'s in the words *reading, writing,* and *learning* all have angles in the lower zone. These show that there is more aggression and determination than one may suspect in Blair's character. In conclusion, this is the writing of a thinking man, with coordination, rhythm, originality, and intelligence—Blair's writing has real flair!

3. *Barbara Bush: Former First Lady*   Barbara Bush is a bit more original in her writing style. She is very determined, aggressive, and self-sufficient, and the letters are upright. She is a thinking type, not emotional. She takes care of business, is very focused, and has extremely wide spaces between words. These wide spaces also illustrate her lack of trust (unlike her husband, George Sr., a feeling type).

Barbara is a no-nonsense woman, not readily intimate, and it takes her a while to reveal herself to others. Her writing is largely print script with tall, well-executed letters, typical of one who was educated in a private school. The writing is cool, dry, and isolated. But she is well organized, with attention to details, and a perfectionist.

If you look carefully at her sample from a distance, you'll see a wide, vertical path of space that moves downward. This path is called a river, and it shows that Barbara Bush is very private, unlike her public image. Although she plays a public role, her preference is solitude.

Bush's excellent use of space and high form level indicate great intelligence. Much of her energy and skill, however, has been stifled. She also has a deep understanding of life. She has learned to control and conceal her emotional side, appearing to be an easygoing woman of warmth and sincerity. There is, however, no real warmth in her writing. It is one of responsibility, concern, and obligation. There is also hidden aggression in the writing, which helped the former first lady cope with life's vicissitudes and survive in the jungle of politics. She has finely honed instincts as seen by the simplicity and expediency of the stroke and in the overall space picture. She studies situations and people and has a good memory for bad behavior. Perhaps you can see why Barbara Bush is called the "Silver Fox."

4. *Mia Farrow*   Here is a beautiful example of persona writing. Actress Mia Farrow is very self-involved and greatly concerned about how this writing looks on the page. She knows how to get where she wants to go. As a child, Farrow had polio. She overcame this illness and continued to live a very sheltered life. Her father died at the age of fifty-eight. It is said that each time she married, it was to someone who would take her father's place. Farrow describes herself as very dependent, seen in the way the letters hug the baseline. Her writing is very careful but filled with fantasy, shown by the immense upper loops and orality. The uprightness shows her determination to keep constant, steady focus.

In the signature, the second loop in the *M* is quite large. This shows her need to be recognized by others. She also has a sense of idealism as seen by the pronounced upper zone. She presents herself as a gentle, fragile creature, as seen in the light strokes and childlike quality to the writing. But she has a lot of rigid angles, and the writing is both round and angular, in places where you do not expect it to be. The rigidity indicates that once you get Farrow on a track, she stays there. In conclusion, Farrow combines dependency and vulnerability with grit and fortitude.

5. *Felix Klein*   We end this exercise with one of my favorite people, my mentor and teacher, the distinguished Felix Klein, who was the founder of the National Society for Graphology, the premier association that teaches Gestalt graphology in the United States.

This writing is a perfect example of garland connection. The garland writer needs harmony, likes to mediate conflict, and tries to see the best in others. Klein had a nurturing spirit and a love for nature and living things. The many words on the page show his love of communication and conversation. His writing has strong movement to the right, which shows his ability to enable and engage others. There are many creative connections here. For example, in the first line, the *s* in *outstanding* connects to the *t* in one stroke; in the word *quality,* the i-dot becomes the first stroke of the *t*; likewise, the *th* in the word *this*—and these are just in the first sentence.

The upright slant shows Klein's desire for self-control and self-discipline. There is a great competence in the simplified form. His integrity is further confirmed by the absence of illegibility, lovely rhythm, and strong sense for form. Every word is legible, which, despite the speed, is a sign of regard for the reader. The legibility also emphasizes his need for communication. The uneven baseline reveals his emotions, but the regularity of the writing style shows he was willing to keep to routines—once he assigned himself tasks, he completed them. The straight left margin shows his respect for learning. He will be remembered for his grace, gentility, and dignity.

*   *   *

If you're interested in taking your study of handwriting analysis to the next level, I recommend you contact Felix Klein's widow:

Janice Klein
National Society for Graphology
250 West 57th Street, Room 2017
New York, NY 10108
(212) 265-1148
Web site: Under construction.

The NSG gives excellent correspondence courses, as well as master classes in graphology, continuing the teachings of Felix Klein.

Of course, if you have any questions or comments, or are interested in consulting with me privately or for your business, feel free to contact me at any time at this address and phone:

Arlyn Imberman
Emerging Image
900 5th Avenue
New York, NY 10021
(212) 759-3058
E-mail: Emergim@aol.com
Web site: Under construction.

Glossary

angle   Connective writing form that contains sharp, straight strokes.

arcade   Connective writing form that look like arches, rounded on the top and open at the bottom, like an upside-down cup.

autograph   Another name for a signature.

baseline   The line on which writing "rests." This line can be visible (when writing is on ruled paper), or invisible (when writing is on un-lined paper).

brain writing   Term coined by Wilhelm Preyer to explain the process of mentally or physically visualizing letters, then transmitting that information to the sensory and motor areas in the brain that control our motor skills. This process is what creates our writing form on paper.

claw   An aggressive, lead-in stroke that is curved like a claw.

club stroke   Pressure that thickens at the ends of letters or words, a graphic metaphor for an emotional outburst.

connectedness   The degree to which letters are joined to one another.

connection   The point at which letters are joined.

connective forms   The styles of the connections between letters. These are garlands, arcades, angles, and threads.

copybook   The penmanship method taught in school.

counterstroke   A stroke that stresses a direction or movement contrary to what is expected. For example, an opening where a closed form should be.

cover stroke   A stroke that lies over, traces, or encircles another stroke or signature and consciously (or unconsciously) conceals it.

crossbar   The horizontal stroke that crosses or sits on top of the vertical stem in the letter *t*.

crossed stroke   When the last stroke of a word or signature crosses back through it.

cursive writing   Writing style in which one letter is joined to the next.

directional movement   The direction that writing goes from the baseline.

disconnected   Writing in which letters are minimally or not joined and almost have the feel of printed writing.

downstroke   The downward movement of a stroke on a page.

extrovert   An individual who expresses energy to the external world.

feeling type   An individual who makes decisions based on emotions.

final   The last stroke on the letter when it is at the end of a word.

fishhook   Little hooks at the beginning or end of a letter or word, which can indicate tenacity, impatience, irritability, or an inability to let go.

form   The writer's chosen writing style.

form level   The quality of the overall pattern of writing by its style, symmetry, simplicity, legibility, creativity, movement, and rhythm.

fullness   The width of letters compared with their height.

garland   Connective writing form in which letters are open at the top and rounded at the bottom, like a cup or *u* shape.

Gestalt   The German word that means "complete" or "whole"; also the name of the German school of graphology founded by Ludwig Klages, which looks at the whole picture of a handwriting sample.

Graphoanalysis   A handwriting analysis system invented by Milton Bunker that identifies basic handwriting strokes and relates them to particular personality traits.

graphology   The study of handwriting.

handwriting analysis   The popular term for graphology.

harpoon   Long, hooked initial stroke that comes from below the baseline and implies hidden aggression or compulsive, negative behavior.

i-dot   The dot that tops the lowercase *i*.

initial stroke   An added stroke at the beginning of the first letter in a word.

introvert   An individual who discharges energy toward his or her internal world.

intuitive type   An individual who believes and relies on information received from his or her own internal or imaginative world.

irregularity   Inconsistency or fluctuation in a writing pattern.

letterform   The unique style with which an individual creates letters.

loops   Circled formations in writing, in either the upper or the lower zone.

lower zone   Writing that hangs below the baseline and usually includes the bottoms of the letters *f, g, j, p. q, y,* and *z.*

margin   The amount of blank space left around writing on a page.

middle zone   Writing that rests on the baseline, which includes the letters *a, c, e, i, m, n, o, r, s, u, v, w,* and *x.*

movement   The trend, rhythm, speed, spacing, and direction of writing.

Myers-Briggs Type Indicator   A personality assessment test developed by the psychologists Katherine Cook Briggs and Isabel Briggs Myers, and based on Carl Jung's personality types, which categorizes individuals and their preferences by sixteen combinations of personality types.

narrowness   Slender letterforms.

overconnected   Writing that is seamless with no breaks at all and the potential for crowding.

paraph   The final stroke in a signature, which can form an underline, swirl, or other embellishment.

pastose   A stroke, usually written with a felt-tipped pen, that is thick and brushlike in texture.

persona writing   An artificial, nonexpressive writng form that is imitative and unspontaneous rather than a natural reflection of the personality of the writer.

personal pronoun *I*   The capital letter *I,* when used to signify the writer.

pressure   The force of the pen on the page. Can be detected by indentations that show on the reverse side of the page.

printed writing   Writing style in which letters are not connected to one another.

Psychogram   A graph developed by Klara Roman that measures character traits in a writer.

regularity   Consistency in a writing pattern.

rhythm   The ease with which the writer expresses the contraction and release of the letters in the writing pattern and stroke.

Sacre Coeur   Writing style taught in French convent schools; a very artificial writing in which the tops and bottoms of letters are covered by the strokes that come before them. This style hides the individuality and innate personality of the writer, though professional graphologists are trained to see through this "mask."

school type   Same as *copybook*—the style of writing taught in school.

script   See *cursive writing*.

sensing type   An individual who believes and relies on information he or she receives from the external world.

signature   The writing of one's name.

simplification   The lack of unnecessary or embellished strokes from a writing form.

size   Overall height and width of writing.

slant   The angle formed by strokes going up from or down to the baseline. Slant direction can be right, left, upright, or variable.

space   The areas visible between lines, words, and letters in a word, as well as margins.

speed   The pace with which words are written.

stroke   The path traced by the pen on paper.

t-bar   The horizontal line that crosses the letter *t*.

thinking type   An individual who makes decisions based on logic.

thread   Connective writing form that is loosely written and usually flat, often resembling a thread.

trend   The horizontal movement of writing.

typology   One of six personality types as defined by Carl Jung, based on how individuals receive, process, and expend their energy. The types are introvert, extrovert, sensate, intuitive, thinking, and feeling.

upper zone   Writing that extends above the baseline and usually includes the tops of the letters *b, d, f, h, k, l,* and *t*.

upstroke   The upward movement of a writing stroke on a page.

variable slant   Writing in which the slant changes.

zones   The three sections—upper, middle, and lower—within each line of writing. (See *lower zone, middle zone,* and *upper zone*).

Graphological Key

A Quick Reference to Handwriting Traits

ANGLE CONNECTION
Willful, tenacious,
intense, controlling.

ARCADE CONNECTION
Reserved, secretive,
formal, conventional.

ASCENDING LINES
Active, ambitious,
optimistic. Reflects
a temporary state of
mind. In some cases,
reflects an attempt
to fight a feeling of
sadness or low spirits.

BASELINE
Steady:
Goal-
oriented,
well centered.

Wavy: Moodiness
and emotional
variability.

CLUB STROKE
Prone to emotional
outbursts, capable of
sarcasm or cruelty.

COMPACT WRITING

Good concen-
tration,
disciplined,
focused, shy.

DESCENDING LINES

Fatigued, sad,
pessimistic, weak-
willed. Reflects
temporary state
of mind.

DISCONNECTED WRITING

Analytical, creative,
intuitive. Can be moody
and unpredictable.

EMBELLISHED WRITING

Ostentatious,
pretentious,
extroverted. Can show
a sense for form and
aesthetics.

FAST SPEED

Active, spontaneous,
quick-thinking, able to
process information
quickly.

FISHHOOK

Tenacious, unable to
let go (of people,
things, or the past).

GARLAND CONNECTION

Flexible, good-natured, tolerant. A mediator who dislikes conflict and discord.

HARPOON

Aggressive, angry, dominating, controlling.

HEAVY PRESSURE

Willful, determined, controlling. Shows intensity and vitality

HIGHLY CONNECTED WRITING

Detail-oriented, organized, logical, realistic.

IRREGULARITY

Rebellious, undisciplined, careless.

LARGE WRITING

Proud, enthusiastic, independent, entrepreneurial. Desires attention and recognition.

LEFT SLANT

Self-focused,
self-protective,
living in the past,
resistant to change.

LEFT TREND

Self-centered,
withdrawn, resisting
authority.

LETTER SPACING

Balanced:
Warm,
adaptable,
open-minded.

Narrow:
Refusal to
reflect or
practice
introspection
on oneself and
life in general.

Wide:
Outgoing, chatty,
spontaneous.

**Space After First
Letter:** Cautious.

Irregular:
Ambivalent.

LINE SPACING

Balanced:
Organized,
with
good
common
sense and
planning
skills.

Narrow: Lacking judgment or self-knowledge.

Wide: Analytic,
well-mannered,
organized, refined.

Irregular: Impulsive, moody, lacks self-confidence.

LOWER ZONE

Material needs,
libido, creativity,
aggression.

MARGINS

It is wiser to analyze the margin solely for aesthetic significance and judge the other character traits from the handwriting itself.

Around the Page

Balanced Around Page:
Orderly, good at planning, well adjusted.

Narrow Margins Around:
Multitasking, doesn't give space to others.

Wide Margins Around: Private, self-protective, shies away from physical contact.

Left Margin

Narrow:
Casual, liking familiarity, careful with money.

Narrowing:
Cautious,
protective,
loses interest
easily.

> hot nor too cold — The sky is grey
> quite humid — This morning I had
> for breakfast — The very good San-Miguel
> baked by the nice german baker —

Wide: High standards, reserved, can be running from the past.

> The packet of samples enclosed is for
> your amusement/edification or whatever.
> Today the pressure is really on; money
> works wonders — gotta find a way to make
> some!

Widening: Impatient, extravagant, enthusiastic about reaching goals.

> Next time you are in town, bring some
> forms for NSG. One gal, Angela Jones,
> called me after the meeting to get your
> address + where she could write for a
> study program. She is seriously interested
> in graphology. We get a mish mash of people

Straight:
Respecting
learning,
education,
culture.

> Thanks very much for the beautiful
> card and the clock. As I have a
> account here in which I deposited th
> housekeeping money Charlie (charlotte)
> while she is in the U.S. I'll deposit it.

Right Margin

Wide: Cautious, oversensitive, fearful of the future.

Widening:
Fearful of
others, shy,
needing
encouragement.

Narrow:
Active,
goal-oriented,
outgoing.

Narrowing:
Eager,
risk-taking.

Straight:
Consistent,
having
self-control.

> *[handwritten text]* erday, and for taking all the ... so our meeting so so many facts so present.

Inconsistent: Uncertain about goals, moody, ambivalent.

> *[handwritten text]* I'm looking forward to fishing and spending some time with you and your new home I'll call to let you know all the details about the flights.

Upper Margin

Narrow:
Informal,
inconsiderate,
lacking respect.

> *[handwritten text]* Dear Roger, Just a short note to "THANK You" for taking the time when you were in L.A. to conduct a mini

Wide:
Modest,
reserved,
respectful.

> *[handwritten text]* Dear Roger — Thank you for spending

Lower Margin

Narrow:
Sentimental,
dreamer,
economical.

Wide: Aloof,
superficial,
emotional or
sexual issues.

Crowded End
of Lines:
Poor at planning,
lacking foresight,
inability to
anticipate.

MEDIUM-SIZE
WRITING

Well adjusted,
realistic,
sociable.

MIDDLE ZONE EMPHASIS

Lives in present, well adjusted, ability to deal with reality and emotions.

> Look forward to seeing you in Ann Arbor. Melt

MODERATELY CONNECTED WRITING

Sharp reasoning skills, good problem solver, adaptable, sociable.

> Well. I've been putting this off for a long time now! I think I'm ready to hear what you have to say about me. I met this man in August of

MUDDY WRITING   Lacking drive, libido.

> removed entire spleen, portion of lower right lung, - spare diaphragm no movement/numbness in legs -

NARROW LETTERS   Inhibited, distrustful.

> the eye and stick to it even when it's hard. If you use and project the power that comes with convictions

NARROW WRITING

Introspective, ability to concentrate, quick thinking, originally introverted but now expressing extrovert behavior.

OVERCONNECTED WRITING   Compulsive, focused, possessing willpower, relies on logic rather than emotions.

OVERLAPPING LINES

Uninhibited, chaotic thinker, inconsiderate.

PARAPHS (Underlines)

Precise, vehement, self-serving.

PASTOSE STROKE

Warm, sensual, hedonistic.

Dr. Polo, a Dr. Armañi Navarro, al Dr. Vargas,

PRESSURE

Normal Pressure: Vital, mature, intelligent.

I'm energy a carrier of simplicity between myself and the world.

Light Pressure:
Delicate, sensitive, lacking stamina.

All is well with my friend

Heavy Pressure:
Driven, determined, committed.

WORLD PEACE !

Very Heavy Pressure:
Angry, frustrated, intense, ill-tempered.

Pressure in Lower Zone Only:
Emphasis on sexual desires.

I know how proud you all feel of her. With every wish for your own great happiness - believe me → Faithfully yours.

PRINTING

Prefering control and clarity.

If time permits, please call me as soon as possible so that we can move forward quickly.

REGULARITY

Disciplined, reliable, good willpower, able to concentrate.

I'm very interested in how you addressed the contents of the attached article.

RHYTHM

Strong:
Stable, steadfast, disciplined.

The rain just can't get me down — I feel so good. The weekend is like a dream now, vivid in my mind's eye and oh so special. I love you! The

Weak:
Disorganized, fickle, lacks self-control.

Coryell & the Eleventh House, fresh from a sold-out week at Max's positively bowled over the audience. It obvious that Coryell

RIGHT SLANT

Taking initiative, goal-oriented, forward thinking.

When faced with a humming

RIGHT TREND   Goal-oriented, adventurous.

A number of American cities have instal

ROUNDEDNESS

Adaptable, sociable, warm, nurturing.

I will take care of your coffee machine on Wed. I hope that's ok. With you I do certainly know to replace things that I brake - But In the same time You should know that it was in

SCHOOL TYPE
  Needs approval,
  avoids taking risks.

participation basic sala

SHARP STROKE
  Focused, articulate,
  analytical.

Michael R. Miller

SIMPLIFIED STYLE   Intelligent, cultured, active, expedient.

I want to think you + at the same time command you on a beautiful

SLOW SPEED
  Precise, careful,
  perfectionist,
  inhibited, lacks
  spontaneity.

Thanks so much for It was really colorful

SMALL WRITING
  Able to concentrate,
  modesty, pragmatic,
  objective.

removed entire spleen, portion of lower right lung, - spare diaphragm no movement / numbness in leg. -

THREAD CONNECTION

Creative, quick thinker, independent. Can also show ambiguity or lack of commitment.

UNEVEN WRITING SIZE

Varying sense of self-worth.

UPPER ZONE EMPHASIS

Ego issues, active imagination.

Yours sincerely,

Ivan F. Boesky
Managing Partner

UPRIGHT SLANT

Self-reliant, disciplined, focusing on present. Needing independence and introspection.

VARIABLE SLANT

Ambivalent, confused.

WIDE WRITING

Vain,
extravagant.

Dear Roger,

I would really love to go back to Google. I think it is one of the most beautiful places to visit.

WORD SPACING   **Balanced:** Balanced, respect for boundaries.

Alas, the spring is upon us. It is warm beautiful and a quite sensation of a soul

Narrow Word Spacing:
Talkative,
outgoing,
confident.

the eye and stick to it even when it's hard. If you use and project the power that comes with convictions then no matter what you face you will be unique and remarkable

Very Narrow Word Spacing:
Impulsive,
dependent

Wide Spacing:
Reserved,
philosophical,
distant.

I have it / I am for Providence Rhode

Very Wide Word Spacing: Shy, lonely, fearing intimacy.

In   Conclusion   we   have   one

Irregular Spacing: Emotionally unstable, impatient, unreliable.

drug use is escapism whether you want to admit it or not.
a person may have spent months, years trying to get help... but
the amount of time one spends trying to get help and the years it
takes to become completely drug free is nothing in comparison.
every junkie ive ever met has fought with it at least 5 years and
most end up fighting for about 15 25 years until finally
they have to resort to becoming a slave to another drug the 12 step
program which is in itself another drug / religion. If it works for
you do it. If your ego is too big start at square one and.
go the psychological rehabilitate way. either way youre got
at least 5 to 10 years of battle ahead of you.

Graphological Worksheet

Date: _____ Name: _____
Gender: Male Female

Circle the traits you see present in the sample you are evaluating.

Handwriting Qualities	Trait Specifics			Meaning
Margins				
Overall:	Balanced	Narrow	Wide	_____
Left Margin:	Consistently Narrow		Narrowing	_____
	Consistently Wide		Widening	_____
	Straight		Irregular	_____
Right Margin:	Consistently Narrow		Narrowing	_____
	Consistently Wide		Widening	_____
	Straight		Irregular	_____
Upper Margin:	Narrow	Wide		_____
Lower Margin:	Narrow	Wide		_____
Spacing				
Line Spacing:	Balanced	Narrow		_____
	Overlapping	Wide	Irregular	_____
Word Spacing:	Balanced	Narrow	Very Narrow	_____
	Wide	Very Wide	Irregular	_____
Letter Spacing:	Balanced	Narrow	Wide	Irregular	_____
	Space after first letter			_____
Baseline	Steady	Wavy		_____
Zones	Upper	Middle	Lower	_____
	Balanced			_____
Size	Small	Medium	Large	_____
	Varying			_____
Connective Form	Garland	Arcade	Angle	_____
	Thread			_____
Strokes	Downstroke	Upstroke		_____
	School Type	Sharp Stroke	Pastose	_____

Handwriting Qualities	Trait Specifics				Meaning
Connectiveness	Moderately Connected	Highly Connected			_____
	Overconnected	Disconnected	Printed		_____
Slant	Right	Left	Upright	Variable	_____
Directional Movement	Right Trend	Left Trend			_____
Rhythm	Strong	Weak			_____
Form	Regular Legible	Irregular/Illegible			_____
Speed	Slow	Well Paced			_____
	Fast	Very Fast			_____
Pressure	Normal	Heavy	Light		_____
Signature					
Form:	Legible	Illegible			_____
Size:	Small	Medium	Large		_____
Emphasis:	First name larger than last name				_____
	Last name larger than first name				_____
	First and last names of equal size				_____
Embellishment:	Crossed	Circled	Underlined		_____
	Other	None			_____
Balance:	Larger than text				_____
	Smaller than text				_____
	Balanced				_____
Typology	Extrovert	Introvert			_____
	Sensing	Intuitive			_____
	Thinking	Feeling			_____

Overall Impression: _____

_____

_____

Conclusion: _____

_____

_____

_____

Code of Ethics for Graphologists

1. The object of this Code of Ethics is to define the rights and responsibilities of graphologists wishing to exercise their profession in accordance with acceptable professional standards and the respective laws of the state in which the graphologist practices.

2. The graphologist is expected to maintain and develop his or her specialized skills by obtaining appropriate professional training. This may be accomplished through such venues as academic seminars, technical training, workshops, or the like. The graphologist is to follow developments in the profession and be aware of the literature relevant to the practice of graphology.

3. The graphologist studies the personality of the writer by examining an original sample of writing. When examining a facsimile or photocopy of the original sample, the graphologist should have accompanying information regarding the pressure. It is further recommended that when giving a report on a faxed or copied sample, a disclaimer be included that the opinion rendered is qualified until such time as an original is made available.

4. The graphologist shall practice only within his or her area of competence or expertise. Consistent with the laws in the state where the graphologist practices, no diagnosis regarding physical or mental health problems will be given unless the graphologist is a psychologist or physician.

5. The work undertaken by the graphologist concerning the human person imposes the respect of moral and professional values. The graphologist must safeguard at all times their own independence, integrity, and sense of humanity. The practice of graphology must be free of racial, gender, religious, or political biases.

6. The graphologist, as with other professionals, shall not use the information obtained from the handwriting to harm the writer, even if the writer is not the client, but a third party. Furthermore, in conveying their findings, the graphologist should specify that the information contained therein is confidential and should be used for professional purposes only. Graphologists who perform

third-party analyses shall request of the client to inform the writer that their handwriting sample is subject to examination by a professional graphologist.

7. The graphologist shall adhere to the highest levels of confidentiality and shall not disclose any information regarding the client without the written release of information signed by the subject/client or by their legal guardian. In accordance with the laws of confidentiality, the report produced by the graphologist shall be provided only to the client supplying the sample. A disclaimer in the report is desirable, stating that, should the legal owner of the report choose to disseminate said written reports further, it would be the sole discretion and responsibility of the owner of such reports.

8. The graphologist shall not disseminate or publish texts or analyses without the written agreement of the interested party or the owner of the document. However, handwriting samples may be used as long as the graphologist respects the anonymity and protects the identity of the writers.

9. Being the sole judge of the worth of the documents submitted to him/her, the graphologist shall reserve the right to refuse to provide an analysis without having to give any reason for doing so. The graphologist shall refuse to express an opinion on a document they know or suspect to be stolen, obtained in violation of any state or federal law, or under other questionable circumstances.

10. Each association or grouping of graphologists, having signed this Code of Ethics, shall undertake to ensure that it is respected and applied by all their qualified members. Each respective association of graphologists signatory to this Code shall establish and maintain a Board of Ethics. The responsibilities of such Board shall be to investigate the complaints made to the Board regarding questionable behavior of the graphologist, meet with the graphologist in question, and render a decision on whether or not any rules of the Code of Ethics have been violated. Such a decision shall be made public by listing the name of the graphologist in the publication of said association, to the local association of attorneys, and to the National Board of Ethics of Graphology.

Recommended Graphology Organizations

United States

National Society for Graphology
250 W. 57th St., Room 2017
New York, NY 10108
(212) 265-1148
Fax: (212) 307-5671
Web site: Under construction.

American Handwriting Analysis Foundation (AHAF)
P.O. Box 6201
San Jose, CA 95150
(800) 826-7774
www.handwritingfoundation.org
E-mail: ahaf@iwhome.com

American Society of Professional Graphologists
2025 Kings Hwy.
Brooklyn, NY 11229
(718) 339-6868
www.aspghandwriting.org
E-mail: questions@aspghandwriting.org

Handwriting Analysis Research Library
Robert E. Backman, Curator
91 Washington St.
Greenfield, MA 01301-3411
(413) 774-4667

Overseas Organizations

United Kingdom

The British Academy of Graphology
Administrative Centre
11 Roundacre
London SW19 6DB
England
+44-181-788-3289
Fax: +44-181-788-4729
www.graphology.co.uk

British Institute of Graphology
24-26 High St.
Hampton Hill, Middlesex TW12 1PD
England
01753 891-241
www.britishgraphology.org
E-mail: contact@britishgraphology.org

The Association of Qualified Graphologists
Collier House
163-169, Brompton Rd.
London SW3 1PY
England
+171 589 4567
Fax: +171 589 8053

Belgium

Association of Belgian Graphologists
4, rue Campenhout
1050 Brussels
071 58 99 24
Fax: 071 58 22 72
www.graphologie-asso.be
E-mail: info@graphologie-asso.
be

The Netherlands

Dutch Graphological Society
Secretariaat N.O.G.
Mw. Mr. L.T.Y.M. van
Mourik-Tjen,
Van Coothweg 1
5371 AB Ravenstein
0486 411808
Fax: 0486 416210
www.grafologie.net
E-mail: grafologiesecr
@grafologie.net

France

Groupement des Graphologues Conseils de France
C/O Monique Riley
49, rue Godot-de-Mauroy
75009 Paris
France
01 42 65 28 28
www.ggcf.fr/sommaire.htm
E-mail: grapho@ggcf.fr

Societe Francaise de Graophologie (SFDG)
5, rue Las Cases
75007 Paris
France
01 45 55 46 94
www.graphologie.asso.fr
E-mail: sfgrapho@
club-internet.fr

Spain

Sociedad Espanola de Grafologia
www.soespgraf.cjb.net

Germany

Professional Association of Certified Graphologists/ Psychologists (PACG)
C/O Helmut Ploog
Rossinstr. 9
D-85598 Baldham near
Munich
Germany
+49 8106-8305
E-mail: dr.ploog@t-online.de

Canada

Association of Graphologists of Quebec
Boîte postale 49004, Succ. de la Colline
Sainte-Foy, (Québec)
G1X 4V2
Montréal: (514) 990-5182
http://iquebec.ifrance.com/agq/
E-mail: assgqc@iquebec.com

Société des Spécialistes en Graphologie du Québec inc. (SSGQ)
120 rue Saint-Olivier, app. 2
Québec (Québec)
G1R 1G1
(418) 624-9315 /
1 866 424-9315
www.graphologiessgq.org
E-mail: luce.boudreau@
sympatico.ca

Institut de Psychographphologie de Montreal Inc.
C.P. 446, suc. Youville,
Montréal, Québec H2P 2V6
(514) 990-0567
http://pages.infinit.net/ipgm/
E-mail: papillonlou@
vidéotron.ca

Italy

A.G.I. Associazione Grafologica Italiana
Scale San Francesco 8 – C.P. 178
60121 Ancona
Italy
071-206100
www.a-g-i.it
E-mail: info@a-g-i.it

Associazione Grafologi Professionisti
p.zza della Mercanzia, 2
40125 Bologna
Italy
051.220304
www.grafologiprofessionisti.com
info@grafologiprofessionisti.it

The Girolamo Moretti Institute of Graphology
Piazza S. Francesco 7,
I 61029 Urbino (PS)
Italy
+39 0722-2639
www.grafologia.it
E-mail: info@grafologia.it

Switzerland

Society of Swiss Graphologists
SGG/SSG
Weinbergstrasse 102
8006 Zürich
01 364 50 52
www.sgg-graphologie.ch
info@sgg-graphologie.ch

Israel

**Israel Society for Scientific
Graphology (SSGI)**
www.graphology.org.il
*(Please note: Web site
is in Hebrew.)*
agraph@bezeqint.net

Bibliography

Adrain, Lorne. *The Most Important Thing I Know*. Kansas City, Mo.: Andrews McMeel Publishing, 1997.

Amend, Karen Kristen, and Mary Stansbury Ruiz. *Achieving Compatibility with Handwriting Analysis*. North Hollywood, Calif.: New Castle Books, 1992.

Bernard, Marie. *Sexual Deviation*. Albany, N.Y.: Whitson Publishing, 1990.

Keirsey, David, and Marilyn Bates. *Please Understand Me: Character and Temperament Types*. Del Mar, Calif.: Prometheus Nemesis Book Company, 1978.

Kristoff, David, and Todd Nicherson. *Predictions for the Next Millennium*. Kansas City, Mo.: Andrews McMeel Publishing, 1998.

Lewinson, Thea Stein, and Joseph Zubin. *Handwriting Analysis*. New York: King's Crown Press, 1942.

Lowe, Sheila. *The Complete Idiot's Guide to Handwriting Analysis*. Indianapolis: Alpha Books, 1999.

McNichol, Andrea, and Jeffrey A. Nelson. *Handwriting Analysis: Putting It to Work for You*. Chicago: Contemporary Books, 1991.

Malone, Michael. *Psychetypes: A New Way of Exploring Personality*. New York: Dutton, 1977.

Martin, Kevin. *Autograph Collector*. Corona, Calif.: Odyssey Publications, 1999.

Nezos, Renna. *Advanced Graphology*. London: Hutchinson, 1989.

Olyanova, Nadya. *Handwriting Tells*. Los Angeles: Wilshire Book Company, 1969.

———. *The Psychology of Handwriting*. Los Angeles: Wilshire Book Company, 1960.

Patterson, Jane. *Sign Here: How Significant Is Your Signature?* London: Ashgrove Press, 1998.

Pulver, Max. *The Symbolism of Handwriting*. London: Scriptor Books, 1994 (translated from the original German edition, 1931).

Roman, Klara. *Handwriting: A Key to Personality*. Columbus, Ohio: SMF Press. 1996.

Saudek, Robert. *Experiments with Handwriting*. New York: William Morrow, 1928.